MW00604045

THE
GREATER
GOOD

Life Lessons from Hawai'i's Leaders

THE GREATER GOOD

Life Lessons from Hawai'i's Leaders

Evan and Kari Leong

**Greater
Good**

Dedicated to our sons,
Buddy and Kolton Leong

ISBN 978-0-9796769-0-1

Library of Congress Control Number: 2007935027

Produced by:
Watermark Publishing
1088 Bishop St., Suite 310
Honolulu, HI 96813
www.bookshawaii.net

Please direct bulk orders and all other inquiries regarding this book to:
Greater Good Books
Telephone: (808) 945-1111
Fax: (928) 563-4428
www.GreaterGoodBooks.com

Printed in Korea

Contents

"Find your passion. Dream big and don't give up!"

Duane Kurisu
Partner
Kurisu & Fergus
Chairman and Chief Executive Officer
AIO Group

ACKNOWLEDGMENTS

Evan & Kari Leong, Co-Founders, Greater Good Inc.

During this year's Greater Good interviews, we were often reminded of our community leaders and trailblazers who have paved the way to make things smoother and easier for all of us. "You did not get here alone," many said. "Think about all of those people who supported you and sacrificed so that you could go to a good school, get a good job, raise a healthy family ..."

We want to take this opportunity to thank the many special people who have guided us through this journey of living to learn. First to Duane Kurisu, who taught us that business is not healthy without the support of the community and the community is not healthy without the support of business. Because of the few minutes you took to explain to Evan the secret to your success, we have revamped our life and thought process. Without your advice and guidance, we would still be chasing the golden ring without a clear path or purpose. Thank you for always being available to listen and to guide and support our journey.

Thank you to our interviewees, who took time out of their busy schedules to share their stories and learning lessons with us. We appreciate your anecdotes, philosophies, stories of celebration and learning experiences. Many have learned from your voices over the radio waves, television, Internet, and now many will learn from your words. In all forms, you're helping our future leaders make positive changes in business while making a difference in our community.

A special thanks to Clint Arnoldus and Central Pacific Bank for believing in us and our vision from the start. Your support allowed us to take our message and stories of Hawai'i's business and community leaders to the global community. Mahalo to Rick Blangiardi and the KGMB9 team for expanding the message to television. Thank you for believing in our growth and ability to become "television people."

A big mahalo to Sara Uemura, Jan Hori, Katherine Nichols, Frank Bridgewater, Don Chapman, Chad Pata, Erika Engle, Ron Nagasawa, Dave Kennedy and Dennis Francis at the *Honolulu Star-Bulletin* and *MidWeek*. Aloha Joan Bennet and the Bennet Group for 2006 PR. Thank you, Cathy and Brian Luke, for always helping; Louis Law for graphics; Lincoln Jacobe for endless support; Edward Sugimoto for our Oceanic column; Don Kim at Sony; Kate and KWME; Nate Smith from Oceanic Time Warner; Emi Anamizu and Madelyn Fukuhara at Core Group One; Richard Lewis at Core Systems Hawai'i; Josh Feldman at Tori Richard; Luke Tucker and Luis Alvisua, our interns; Raynette Tinay and team at C&J Telecommunications and Marsha Nadalin and Marsha Nadalin Salon & Spa. Thanks to PBS Hawai'i for airing the "Greater Good Moments."

An extended thanks to our Philippines Greater Good Team who spent countless hours helping us create this book—Dan-Gil, Jay-R and Davi. The team at Watermark Publishing, especially George Engebretson and Aimee Harris, for your patience and incredible eyes to help edit and create the attractive layout of our book.

And last, but not least, the people who have supported us continuously and unconditionally, our family. Mom, Dad and Popo Leong and Mom and Dad Okino, without your guidance, love and support, we could not have made it this far. You have allowed us to grow and develop as individuals and have sacrificed a lot to help us throughout our lives. Although you have not been quoted directly in this book, you have shared a lot of wisdom over the years. Most of all, your voices live in our minds and hearts, speaking loudly of the morals and values that make us good human beings. To our siblings, Tishya, Jon, Darin, Lisa, Kyle and Jocelyn, thank you for always encouraging us and supporting us. You have sacrificed a lot to help us succeed in all we do.

To our boys, Buddy and Kolton, we love you more than we can express. You have brought so much love and laughter into our relationship and you have veered us away from working all the time. We hope this book will be useful for you throughout your lives. We hope that you will use the knowledge to be successful in whatever you choose to do and whatever path you take. Just remember to be passionate, be a good person, say your prayers and never forget that we love you to the moon and back.

FOREWORD

by Mufi Hannemann, Mayor of Honolulu

My life is guided by a number of precepts—I've dubbed them "Mufi's Maxims"—that set forth many of the ideals and everyday practices I apply in my responsibilities as mayor of the City and County of Honolulu, and which I've encouraged the members of my cabinet to follow as they go about their duties.

These maxims were not a revelation, not some creation whipped up in a burst of creative energy. Rather, they were gathered and refined through years of living and work experience in Hawai'i and around the world, both positive and negative, much like the ideas and thoughts being shared in *The Greater Good: Life Lessons from Hawai'i's Leaders.*

One of them is, "Leave this a better place than you found it." It's a maxim I've followed throughout my career in public service. Public service, for me, has never been about power or prestige or the usual trappings of elected office. It has always been about using God's gifts to make this a better place, to serve and sacrifice for others, to contribute to the greater good; these have been motivating factors in driving me to public service and to creating the Pacific Century Fellows leadership program.

It hasn't been easy, believe me. Ours is a democracy, not an autocracy. People have a say in the directions and goals of our city, the state and the nation, and they're not hesitant about expressing those views. It's a near-impossibility to get a group of people to agree on what they want to eat for lunch, let alone getting them to agree on a complex issue. But I think that if your intentions are good, you keep the debate open and honest, and you're motivated by a sincere desire to make a meaningful contribution, then you can achieve great things and make this a better place than you found it.

There's one more point to be made about the purpose of this book. The day I received my high school diploma, I was on top of the world. Surrounded by my parents, brothers and sisters, relatives and friends; oodles of flower leis; a wonderful high school education behind me and a Harvard University degree before me, I couldn't have felt more assured of my place on earth.

My father, Gustav, a soft-spoken, humble immigrant who had labored tirelessly without complaint for many years and who helped my mother, Faiaso, to raise their seven children, then stepped up to me to put a lei around my neck. As he did, he whispered in my ear, "Son, you know nothing."

I had just completed six years at one of the finest college prep schools in the United States, earned the Iolani Headmaster's Award, been named an all-star in basketball and football, completed a term as student body president and been accepted to Harvard, Yale, Princeton, Brown, Cornell and Stanford—and I still knew nothing, in my dad's eyes. In essence, he was encouraging me to be humble, stay focused on education and keep thirsting for knowledge.

My Dad's Dictum, if you will, has stayed with me for the past 35 years. Indeed, we know nothing. There's always more to learn, a new idea on the horizon, a different opinion, a unique perspective to add to the mix. The people who have generously shared their unique wisdom, experiences, and thoughts in *The Greater Good* tell us that learning is a life long journey, and that we should continue to learn from the experience and wisdom of others.

We can all be grateful to Evan and Kari Leong for their commitment to the betterment of our community, our state and our nation and their inspiring work for the good of all.

INTRODUCTION
Evan Leong, Chief Executive Officer, Greater Good Inc.

I hate doing yard work but I'm fascinated with farming. I have no desire to be a farmer, yet I love the potential in farming—taking a little seed and growing it into a productive crop to be harvested year after year.

I learned this sense of providence in the same yard where my grandfather planted his first tree. My Gung Gung (Chinese for grandfather) was a Chinese-American who worked extremely hard to educate and provide for his family. In his free time he planted and cared for many fruit trees in our yard. We have five mango trees, six lychee trees, orange trees, lemon trees, pomelo trees and several others.

I wasn't there to watch him prepare the ground, plant the seeds and nurture the growth, but I definitely enjoyed eating the fruit. Generations have been raised at my Gung Gung's home in Mānoa Valley, that verdant suburb of Honolulu. It has been more than 20 years since my Gung Gung passed away, but the fruit from the seeds he planted, almost a century ago, is still enjoyed by our family.

Fruit trees weren't the only thing he passed down to the generations. My Gung Gung also taught us important lessons in life based on his own experiences. These experiences were the "seeds of knowledge" of his life, which shaped him into who he was and later helped shape the people that we have become.

Each experience is like a small seed of knowledge. A fruit tree can feed people for generations to come, and the same goes for these trees of success. The beauty of seeds of knowledge is that they don't have to be our own.

I once heard at a seminar: "Find someone who has what you want. Think how they think. Do what they do and you'll get what they have."

That is what this book is all about. In the past year and a half, my wife, Kari, and I have interviewed hundreds of the most prominent business, community and government leaders in Hawai'i and around the world to find out how they think and what their life experiences have been. We are on a quest to find the very best "seeds of knowledge" that these people are planting.

On this journey, we found the same underlying core values mentioned over and over again in the interviews. Even though the stories and experiences are quite different, they're each built on the same basic foundations.

Our goal at Greater Good is to be a vehicle to pass along values that were a part of each leader's foundation for success, to help you create your own definition of a successful life.

While conducting the interviews, we also noticed something intriguing. No matter what preconceived notion we had of our interviewees, we always came out of the interviews with a different perspective. We realized that many of these successful people started out like you and I and developed into high achievers. Childhood pictures are under each of the quotes as a reminder that we all start off as children and our choices and decisions along the way make up who we become.

While each person has his or her own definition of success, we can all agree that we'd like to live a fulfilling life. The good news is that life can be even better than what we expect, if we know what to focus on. The main point is to climb the right "ladder of life." Many people climb the ladder of life and reach the top only to realize that they've been on the wrong ladder.

In the Adam Sandler movie *Click*, Sandler's character is asked, "Remember the leprechaun? The one from the cereal ad. He's always chasing the pot of gold at the end of the rainbow, but when he gets there, at the end of the day, it's just corn flakes."

As it turns out, what was first envisioned as a success-in-business book has become a book on life itself. It's a book about making our lives and making a difference. It's about finding the pot of gold instead of the corn flakes. And it all starts with finding our purpose, which is where we begin …

*"Sometimes you cannot see
with your eyes (therefore)
you have to look inside here;
meaning close to your
chest in your heart.
And navigate with your heart."*

Nainoa Thompson
Navigator and Sail Master of the Hōkūleʻa
TRUSTEE AT KAMEHAMEHA SCHOOLS

1

WHAT'S YOUR PURPOSE?

1

WHAT'S YOUR PURPOSE?

Evan Leong, Chief Executive Officer, Greater Good Inc.

I was waiting in line at the airport one day, when I overheard the ticket agent ask the person in front of me for her ticket. She responded that she hadn't bought one yet, but that she had a voucher for a free ticket and wanted to redeem it. When the agent asked where she wanted to go, she said, "I'm not sure. Why don't you choose a place for me?"

I know this sounds silly, but this is how many of us live our lives. We may have a ticket to live our life, but we often let others choose the destination.

Mike May, CEO of Hawaiian Electric Company, Hawai'i's largest utility, said it best:

"If you don't have a plan, you're going to be part of somebody else's."

This is how I lived my life for many years. I plodded along with no real destination, and grew frustrated because I wasn't getting where I thought I should be. I'd let someone else tell me what my destination should be and just headed in the direction they set. I realize now that I wasn't doing what I was supposed to be doing—pursuing the goals I should have been following—but I did it anyway. I was not in control of my life's destination. I had not yet discovered my purpose.

Finding our purpose is about finding our destination in life. I asked myself:

What is my life really supposed to amount to?
What contribution am I supposed to make?
Why am I here?
When I die, will I have accomplished what I was meant to accomplish?

These are questions that I think a great deal about, and one day I received the answers: that my purpose is to inspire as many people as possible and to help them make a positive difference in their lives. To empower people with tools to make changes themselves—the proverbial "give a man a fish, you feed him for a day; teach a man how to fish, and you feed him for a lifetime." To make the world a better place through tangible solutions. To use business as a tool to make an impact on our local, national and global community. It is my purpose to do these things in whatever time I'm allowed here on earth.

While others can help us, our real purpose is a personal calling that can only be discovered and determined by each of us individually. Our parents can tell us to go to school, get good grades and get a certain job. Our teachers can tell us what to be when we grow up. Friends can tell us one thing and the media can tell us another. But here's the dilemma: If we listen to everyone under the sun except ourselves, we inevitably allow our destination to be set by others. Is it any wonder why at that point we feel we've strayed off course? Then frustration and confusion set in, and we either accept that this is how it's going to be or we decide to make a change.

In 2004 I attended 12 funerals. In 2005, a close friend's wife was diagnosed with cancer at the age of 40. At the time, this couple's three boys were all under seven years old. She nearly died several times and I saw first-hand how quickly, and suddenly, life can end. I decided to make a change. And once I consciously identified my purpose, my whole life was transformed.

There's a lot of time to think about life—and death—while you're sitting at a funeral. A funeral can be a celebration of life or a reflection of unfulfilled potential. And while no one ever says anything negative in a eulogy, I can't help but wonder:

Did this person fulfill their purpose?

Why were they here?

Did they make a difference that will have an impact now that they are gone?

Did they live the life they were meant to live?

I wondered how a eulogy would sound if it were written for what a person's life could have been, instead of what it was. I wondered what my eulogy would be if I died suddenly? Would I have lived the life I was supposed to live? I started thinking about all the accomplishments that I thought were important, all the accolades and ego-building materializations. But in the end I could only think of whether or not I became the best I could be at that moment, and if I'd helped anyone else besides myself? My purpose and destination became clear, and I am happy to say that I am finally pursuing it.

When my time comes to leave this world, I aim to have done everything I could to inspire a eulogy like this:

"Evan Leong achieved his life's purpose. He lived every minute with passion. He made a long-lasting, positive impact on his family, his friends and his community."

I hope that the stories and insights in these pages will help educate, motivate and inspire you to discover your own purpose, so that your eulogy reflects what life can be when it is lived to its maximum potential.

"The only strategy in life is to find something you were meant to do, and if you love it you're going to do it well. When you wake up in the morning you have to say, 'Man, I can't wait to go to work.'"

Marc C. Tilker
President and Chief Executive Officer
BEI Hawai'i and HT&T Truck Center

Go Home

Jeffrey Watanabe, Non-Executive Chair of Hawaiian Electric Industries and Founding Partner of Watanabe Ing & Komeiji

During law school, I worked under the patronage of U.S. Senator Daniel Inouye. At the time, he was a 44-year-old senator who had never lost an election. After law school, I was considering a job in Washington. As luck would have it, I was with the Senator late one night awaiting a vote. He asked me what I was going to do when I finished law school. I told him about possibly staying in Washington.

"Go home," he said. "You owe a lot of people."

"What do you mean?" I asked.

"You've had a good education and have been provided many opportunities. You didn't do that all by yourself, you know. Someone decided you were worthwhile and was willing to work hard so that you could have these opportunities. That's an obligation you need to pay back."

That was a long time ago, but the Senator's advice is as valid today as it was then. Many of us had immigrant grandparents, parents, uncles, aunts, friends, professional colleagues and communities who struggled to provide opportunities for generations that followed. That needs to be recognized.

Once I returned to Hawai'i, fulfilling that obligation turned out to be both gratifying and fun. Interestingly, I believe it also significantly helped my business career. Fulfilling my obligations should have always been part of my life's mission, but in my case, it was really driven by people wiser than I.

In 1971, Jeffrey Watanabe co-founded Watanabe Ing & Komeiji, LLC, one of the leading law firms in Hawai'i. He is the non-executive chairman of the board of Hawaiian Electric Industries, a Fortune 1,000 company that supplies 93 percent of Hawai'i's energy needs, and is also on the boards of Alexander & Baldwin and a number of private companies in Hawai'i and the mainland U.S. Actively engaged in the non-profit sector, Jeff is a trustee of Sesame Workshop in New York, the Consuelo Zobel Alger Foundation headquartered in Honolulu and Manila, and The Nature Conservancy of Hawai'i. He has served on the Smithsonian National Board as well as The Nature Conservancy's Board of Governors.

*"Get out there and experience life.
Usually a calling will find you.
You just have to keep your eyes open
to recognize it when it comes.
Don't follow the standard ways
of doing things. Keep your mind open.
Ask your heart what you want to do
because too much of life nowadays
is a little bit too preprogrammed."*

Ed Case
U.S. Congressman, Hawai'i (2002-2007)
UNITED STATES CONGRESS

Be True to Yourself

Gail Mukaihata Hannemann, Chief Executive Officer, Girl Scouts of Hawai'i

World War II shaped the lives of not just my parents, but my entire family, which is the case for a lot of people. My parents were high school age during the war, and both of them were interned. That type of experience changes you as a human being and helps you to prioritize what is important.

As I get older, I have come to really appreciate how my parents brought us up. There were four girls and we were raised in a very traditional Japanese community, which had its pluses and its minuses. The plus was clearly the strong family connection and the values. The minus was that if you didn't fit quite into what was considered honorable or respectable, especially in professions, then you could be in a difficult situation.

Gail Mukaihata Hannemann is the CEO of The Girl Scouts of Hawai'i and the First Lady of the City and County of Honolulu. Just prior to joining the Girl Scouts, Gail served as vice president of corporate development for SMS Inc., one of Hawai'i's premier research and marketing firms. She spent more than 15 years in Washington D.C. as a congressional aide and professional staff member of the U.S. House of Representatives prior to moving to Hawai'i in 1992. Gail is the past chair of the Hawai'i Arts Alliance and serves on the board of the Children's Alliance of Hawai'i, a non-profit organization dedicated to making life better for sexually and physically abused children and their families living on the island of O'ahu.

Regardless, my parents told my sisters and me to do whatever we wanted in life—something that was interesting and important to us. For example, my older sister became a linguist, and she's working with educational technology now. The sister younger than me studied to be a dietician at a time when there were very few Asian women in the field, and then my youngest sister grew to be an artist. We all took non-traditional paths.

The thing that I remember most about my parents is that they were always caring about others. They always told us that—because of their circumstances when they were held in Japanese camps during World Word II—people did things out of the goodness of their heart. When they left the camp, my mother went to New York, and then to Philadelphia to get her education. My dad went elsewhere. They both recall how people took them in and did things to care for them—and that is what they have always taught us to do.

Not long ago, my aunt told me a story about a day that she had experienced with my mom. They were outside of their home unloading the car after coming home from a trip together. Busily unloading their things, they noticed a strange car pull up to the house with a couple and a child.

My aunt asked my mom, "Do you know these people?"

"I don't think so," she replied.

But they were clearly coming to talk to my mom. Of course, my aunt was a little concerned and just stood there as they approached my mom.

They said, "We just wanted to come by and thank you."

My mom was puzzled and asked, "Why?"

The lady said, "You probably don't remember, but it was about six years ago and we came to buy your car. We were just getting started and I was pregnant."

She continued, "We didn't have much money, but we had to move. Out of the kindness of your heart, you just gave the car to us."

These people came back to thank my parents for giving them a break in life, because that made all the difference in the world to them as they got their start. This is just one example of acts of kindness that my sisters and I lived with all the time. Our parents taught us not to just look at ourselves, and also to never look at the initial circumstances. We need to look at our life in a fuller context to give it meaning. At the end of the day life is about people. To give to others—that's where the richness of life lies. Get involved not in other people's business, but in other people. Help enrich other people's lives; it's really important.

*"I like to ask people
what they want written
on their tombstones.
For myself, I would like
to have written,
'He made a difference,'
i.e., I would like to think
that during my lifetime
I made a difference in making
the world a little bit better."*

John Dean
Managing General Partner
STARTUP CAPITAL VENTURES

Bringing Honor Home

Daniel K. Inouye, Senator, United States Senate

I was the eldest son in the family, and in my generation that made a difference. My father was the eldest; my grandfather was the eldest; in fact, I was the seventh generation of first-borns. My grandparents worked in the field on Kaua'i and my father began his education at 14. So they looked upon me as the oldest son to do something big with my life, to do something that would make them proud. I was brought up with that sense. Even from an early age I remember being told, "Never dishonor your family."

It's rather difficult to tell my son today to "never dishonor your family," but in my generation it was a common phrase. "Don't dishonor us. Don't bring any shame to us."

This stuck with me through my life, and then when I was 17, Pearl Harbor was attacked. I soon found out that I was an enemy alien because of a decree of our government. My parents were Japanese and as a result, I could not wear the uniform of this land. I, too, wanted to protect our country but had to wait. Finally in early 1943, the authorities opened the doors and my friends and I volunteered for the Army. I served in the military as an 18-year-old private; I became a sergeant, then eventually a lieutenant and then was promoted to captain.

The big day for me was April 21, because on this day I received my last battle wound. I have vague memories of the moment, because I just rushed the hills with adrenaline flowing. According to witnesses, I was shot in my right elbow and my arm just about fell off. With my good left hand, I picked up and threw the grenade that had been clutched in my

Senator Daniel K. Inouye is the U.S. Senate's third most senior member. In 1959, Inouye won election to the U.S. House of Representatives as Hawai'i's first congressman. Elected to the Senate in 1962, he is serving his seventh consecutive term. In 1943, the 18-year-old Inouye enlisted in the U.S. Army's 442nd Regimental Combat Team, the famed "Go For Broke" regiment. He spent 20 months in Army hospitals after losing his right arm. Inouye was honored with the Distinguished Service Cross (the second highest award for military valor), Bronze Star, Purple Heart with oak cluster and 12 other medals and citations. His Distinguished Service Cross was upgraded to a Medal of Honor, the nation's highest award for military valor.

right hand. Then I picked up my gun and I started to charge. I also had gunshot wounds in my stomach area and right leg.

In World War II, the battles were so intense and large that the casualty rates were in the hundreds of thousands. The field hospitals weren't able to accommodate the wounded and we had no helicopters. In my case, I was evacuated at 3 p.m. and I got to the field hospital at midnight; it took nine hours. When I reached the hospital, there were a bunch of people on stretchers. A small crew of physicians and attendants came along to look at us and rate our status. They pointed to us and said, "Tent No. 1, tent No. 2 and tent No. 3." In other words, tent 1: treat them right away, tent 2: take it easy because this one can last a long time, and tent 3: forget it, that's someone on the verge of death.

I was assigned to tent No. 3. Eventually, the chaplain came by and said, "God loves you."

"I'm certain he loves me. But I'm not ready to see him yet," I replied.

He looked at me and said, "You know, I believe you."

"Yes, I got a whole life ahead of me," I remarked.

He called in the staff and said, "Take him to tent No. 1."

I was immediately moved and had 17 transfusions. The crew did not make a mistake in moving me. But if they hadn't looked after me for a couple of hours, I think I would have just faded away.

While recovering in the military rehab center I was able to reflect upon my service to our country and the government's power. I began to realize that the government made a lot of decisions, and one of the most difficult decisions was going to war. There were other decisions that affected all of our lives—education, health conditions, environment, etc. I felt that as a U.S. citizen, I did my part in protecting our country. But I wanted to do more.

I was wounded four times before getting out of the service. When I was released, I felt that I should do something to help people. Now, that may sound high and mighty, but I meant it. After spending time in the military, watching my friends die or get wounded, I couldn't see myself going back to the plantation way of life.

I remembered a conversation I had with my friend, retired Senator Bob Dole, while we were in rehab, regarding his plans once he returned home. He had his life all planned out. Bob told me that he wanted to make a difference in people's lives and he shared how government was going to help him do it. He was going to study law and run for office to become a senator. Though I had planned to become a doctor, which was now out of the question, I decided that Bob's plan sounded good for me as well. To the chagrin of my folks, because politicians were not highly regarded at that time (and in some quarters they're still not highly regarded) I went to law school and became an assistant prosecutor for one year. Then I ran for the Territorial Legislature and won.

In 1959, Hawai'i became part of the United States of America. I was honored to be elected as Hawai'i's first Congressman and looked forward to seeing my friends, like Bob Dole.

When I was sworn in as a member of the Senate in 1962, my father came along. We were at lunch at that time with the majority leader, Mike Mansfield, whom I got along with very well. A telephone call came in and Mike answered the phone and said, "Dan, the President wants to speak with you."

I picked it up, "Yes, Mr. President."

"I hear your father's in town."

I said, "Yes, sir."

"Why don't you bring him around?"

I said, "I'd love to."

"When can you do that?"

I said, "I'm free now."

"Then bring him around."

So I took my father to the White House to meet President John F. Kennedy. My father was in absolute awe. Being from the plantation, he never imagined the opportunity to be in the White House, nor meet the President of the United States.

Once we were finished with our visit, the Press Corps was waiting. All of the cameras were focused on us as we exited because I had just become a new senator.

The press asked me, "Can you tell us about your meeting with the President? Did you discuss home rule and civil rights?"

I said, "No, this was my father's meeting—not mine. So you better interview him."

My father looked at the camera and he said, "I can die now!"

The newspaper people were stunned.

He then continued by saying, "I've just seen the President of the United States, I've seen my son become a United States Senator. I can die now."

It was at that moment that I knew my father was proud of me and I had fulfilled his dream of honoring my family. But it isn't all about that. I had fulfilled my own dream of loving my work, helping to make a difference in people's lives and being a part of the government's decisions that impact us all in a positive way.

*"I knew, from the way that
I was raised, that I needed
to be involved in the community.
It's part of my being,
it's part of who I am."*

Crystal K. Rose
Partner
BAYS, DEAVER, LUNG, ROSE & HOLMA ATTORNEYS AT LAW

Plantation Lessons

Duane Kurisu, Partner, Kurisu & Fergus, and Chairman
and Chief Executive Officer, aio Group

When I was growing up on the Hilo Coast, words and actions always came from the heart. Later on, I was taught in business school that when you calculate correctly, you get the right answer. That was a real transition for me—someone who did things from the heart had to learn to be calculating and methodical. Now I've come full circle: I realize that while you do have to make decisions based on the facts, you also need to let your intuition guide you—that important decisions can still come from the heart.

In the plantation towns back then, values like trust, respect, honesty and gratitude were a way of life. That's really the only way it could be when everyone knew everyone else—the kids, the teachers, the postmaster, the village peddlers. If a storekeeper gave you too much change, you went back and returned it. If people were older than you, you always addressed them as "Mr." or "Mrs." It was friends helping friends, people helping people.

Raised in the Big Island plantation town of Hakalau, Duane Kurisu today is owner or part-owner of the San Francisco Giants, the *Honolulu Star-Bulletin* and *MidWeek*, ESPN Radio 1420 AM, PacificBasin Communications, Watermark Publishing, the Punaluʻu Bake Shop and several other companies, many of them under the corporate umbrella of The aio Group. A University of Hawaiʻi graduate, he co-founded his first company, Kurisu and Fergus, in his late 20s to develop and manage commercial real estate properties in Hawaiʻi and on the mainland. Duane also established the Hawaiʻi Winter Baseball League, the first professional baseball organization made up of multinational teams and players.

These days, it seems that many of us have lost or forgotten those basic small-town values. And that's a mistake, especially as we try to deal with the many new challenges of a fast-changing, high-tech world. If we ignore where we've been and how we got here, any solutions to today's challenges will be shallow and short-lived. Unless we keep the old ways alive, our children's generation may never benefit from what we learned about building strong family and community values.

The best way to do this, of course, is to teach by example—to show our children that we must be good people first and that all the other good things will naturally follow. That real satisfaction in life comes from within. And that yesterday's basic human values are the catalyst for creating tomorrow's solutions.

When we were children, we lived our lives with abandon. We ran that race, we skipped rope, and we learned to ride that bike with all of our might. Being fat or skinny, or slow or uncoordinated, didn't really matter. These supposed limitations were put aside as we just went out and *did* it, whatever the activity. In those moments, who we were and what we did became one and the same.

As adults, we are also capable of doing remarkable things if we just let ourselves be ourselves. Most of us lose sight of one basic truth: that human beings are divine. So if we seek inspiration in our lives and act with our hearts, we really can't go wrong. As we face life's challenges and opportunities, who we are will dictate what we do. Whether we're dealing with friends and family or trying to make the right business decisions, it is who we are that will determine the outcomes, in both our personal and professional lives.

Therefore, when we reflect upon our purpose in life and whether we've chosen the right path, we should first ask ourselves a couple of questions. Am I the best person that I can be? Have I lived my life with all my might? These are the questions that guided the plantation workers and the children of plantation workers. These are the questions that should guide us today.

"Is the world a better place for me having been here?"

Nate Smith
President and Chief Executive Officer
OCEANIC TIME WARNER CABLE

The "Why" Question

David Carey, Chief Executive Officer, Outrigger Enterprises

During my senior year in high school, my grandfather passed away. I attended his funeral and had a chance to read through cards and letters from secretaries, railroad porters, janitors and mid-level executives, all of whom he had touched in some way. Reading through these personal notes taught me about a part of his life—his business life—of which I had known nothing. Through the eyes of others, I was inspired by his life to go into business and reach out to others and to the community in which I live.

The grandfather I knew was a rotund chap who was always around at Christmas and Thanksgiving. He was a wonderful man but I really had no appreciation of his professional side. When he passed away, I was struggling with my own career direction. I was being recruited by several colleges to play golf, but I had applied to one excellent school that I really wanted to attend.

While trying to decide where I would go, I began thinking about my grandfather and how, as a businessman, he was able to make such a difference in other people's lives. At this point, I regretted not having gotten to know that side of him. It made me say to myself, "You know, I have some talent. It would be a waste for me not to use it, make something of myself, step up to the challenge and, like him, try to make a positive impact on the lives of those around me."

I decided to go to Stanford University, foregoing the golf scholarships. I later wrote on my law school

David Carey is CEO of Outrigger Enterprises. He earned a bachelor's begree in electrical engineering from Stanford University, and a J.D., cum laude, and a master's degree in business administration, with distinction, from Santa Clara University. David is a member of numerous business and community organizations, including Punahou School board of trustees, James Campbell Company board of directors, Hawai'i Business Roundtable, Chamber of Commerce of Hawai'i Military Affairs Council, Air Force Chief of Staff Civic Leaders Group, the Foundation for the Asia-Pacific Center for Security Studies, Blood Bank of Hawai'i board of directors, Honolulu Festival board of directors, Chief Executives Organization, Hawai'i Hotel & Lodging Association, Hawai'i State Bar Association, Urban Land Institute and the Young Presidents' Organization. He is an avid golfer, an occasional tennis player and a retired soccer player.

applications that I wanted to practice law for a while, gain some business experience and then run a company someday.

Knowing the path I had ahead of me, I was focused on living my life and fulfilling the mission inspired by my grandfather. It seems as if, along the way, things just fell into place as they were meant to.

In college, I met a girl from Hawai'i. While we were dating, she asked, "Why don't you come for a visit to Hawai'i?"

It sounded like a great idea, so before my senior year I came to O'ahu for a visit. I loved the place. A group of us were sitting out on a sea wall one warm night, with the moon hanging about 35 degrees over the water, waves breaking in, the breeze blowing gently through the palms, and I asked, "Gee, is it like this all the time?" Everyone looked at me like, "Well yeah, of course, what do you expect?" So I asked my girlfriend's dad, who ran several hotels in Hawai'i, "I'm graduating from college soon. Is there any chance I could come back and get a job and just hang out for a while?"

I had no idea about the family business at the time since we were just dating. Her father was very kind and gave me my first job out of college. My very first assignment was at the front desk at what was then the Outrigger East Hotel. At the time, there were only about a dozen hotels in the system. After about a year or so of hotel work, I continued on the path I had charted and went off to graduate school, got a law degree and an MBA. Then, as I'd planned, I practiced law for a while.

I eventually made it back to Hawai'i to marry that girl. I ended up working for her father again and learned how to lead people, lead a company, and most importantly, lead by giving back to the community that does so much for our business. I was eventually named president and CEO of Outrigger Enterprises, which was a scary thing for me. Although I didn't always know if my daily business decisions were the right ones, I had to take chances and find out for myself.

One thing I did know was that I had a knack for working with people and "reading" them. To begin understanding an employee's philosophy, I spend a lot of time with new hires to understand how they think, how they process a problem, how they approach it. In turn, they begin to understand where I'm coming from, too.

Most people who work for me are very bright and capable. But I look for team players first. I have a saying: "If you're not a team player, you're not going to play on my team."

I don't care how talented you are, there are lots of competent people in the world. So why not have a group of executives who are not only good at what they do, but who like what they do and enjoy working with other people? Competence is very important, of course, and so is intelligence, but the ability to work together is absolutely key. That's the formula for a winning team, and that's probably the most important thing I've learned about leading.

The other thing that has helped me attract great people is being able to answer what I call the "Why?" question. In other words, "Why are we here? Why are we doing what we do?" I believe that if you can answer that question for competent and capable employees, they'll do an excellent job with "what" to do. They won't need me to be there every moment saying, "Do this, do that." I have a stable executive team, and we also have tremendous stability in our line ranks. I believe this is because the people on our team understand their purpose, and that motivates them like nothing else can.

At the same time, it has always remained clear to me what my own purpose is to lead in a way that touches people, that makes a positive impact on my community … and that would make my grandfather proud.

*"My father told me
on my 21st birthday:
The cosmic dust that
you borrow from the universe,
give it back in brighter coin
than you received."*

Mike McCartney
Chairman
THE DEMOCRATIC PARTY OF HAWAI'I

Find Your Purpose

Susan Page, Founder, Susan Page Modeling and Freeze Frame Studios

It's important to find your purpose. Rick Warren's book *The Purpose Driven Life* made this notion universally popular. But it's true—especially before starting your own business. You need to look deep inside before jumping into something as all-consuming as running a business. You need to be sure that it's really something that works not only for you but for all the people around you: your family and extended family.

When you do go into business, you're responsible to it, just like you are to your family. During my business years, I was spread thin. My children needed me, and my business needed me. There were always difficult choices to make about time and priority. I wasn't prepared for the responsibility I felt for my staff and customers—not to mention meeting state regulations and deadlines. Sometimes it was overwhelming.

That's the downside. There are many upsides to business: a sense of providing a service or product that's needed, providing employment for people, a sense of satisfaction from creating something that is successful, being your own boss, learning and forging wonderful relationships.

My advice is to be cautious, but optimistic. Be educated and prepare as much as possible, then go full throttle ahead. As clichéd as it may sound, if nothing is ventured, certainly nothing can be gained. Be passionate about it.

Being in business reminds me of what U2's lead singer, Bono, said about his humanitarian work in Africa. You shouldn't look at helping people in Africa as a burden. Instead look at it as an adventure. Everything in life should be an adventure, right?

Susan Page is the founder of Susan Page Modeling and Freeze Frame Photo Studios and is the vice president of marketing for Coffee Enterprises, Inc. Susan became a busy emcee, guest radio host and public speaker after selling her modeling and fashion photography businesses in 1993. She has been a weekly columnist for Oʻahu's *MidWeek* newspaper for 14 years, writing on current events and lifestyle. Susan co-hosted the Kapiʻolani Children's Miracle Network telethon and specials for 22 years and currently serves as a director on the boards of the Kapiʻolani Health Foundation and Women In Need, and is vice chair of the National Board of the North American humanitarian faith-based organization Heart for Africa.

Besides business, another adventure for me has been an association with Kapiʻolani Medical Center for Women & Children. Way back in 1984, I got involved with the Kapiʻolani Children's Miracle Network and have been an on-air host for 22 years as well as on the board of directors for the Kapiʻolani Health Foundation for the last eight years. Seeing the amazing work the hospital does in our state for the tiniest preemie babies and children with life-threatening diseases or injuries keeps me involved. Children's issues are vitally important because children often have no advocates. They can't speak for themselves, so we need to be there for them.

Most recently I have been involved with the African community. I believe there is just such a grave and dire need there beyond what we can even imagine here in Hawaiʻi and across the United States. Our greatest needs here are the least of theirs.

When I was a child growing up in Texas, our church supported a missionary family. The family worked and lived in Kenya. On a rare visit to Texas, they came to our home, and I had the chance to hear their spell-binding stories of Africa. From that point on I dreamed of going, but I had no idea it would happen.

Then, finally, about five years ago my husband and I went to South Africa on a business/pleasure trip. After an exciting four days at a game preserve, I decided to take a tour into the Soweto township to see where the 4 million black South African victims of apartheid lived. I saw stunning abject poverty, the reality of what life had been under the cruel practice of depriving native Africans opportunities for education, jobs and futures. I knew there was more to see than the African luxury game parks. I left Africa heartbroken but without any hope of knowing what I could do to help. I returned to Hawaiʻi but always kept those experiences in my mind.

Five years later I had an opportunity to get involved in mission work in Africa through my church, First Presbyterian Church of Honolulu. One Sunday in spring of 2005, renowned theologian and author of *The Prayer of Jabez*, Dr. Bruce Wilkinson spoke and challenged our congregation, "Come to Africa with me to help feed the hungry and the children, the most vulnerable among them, as we're called to do as Christians." I found myself signing with his organization called Dream for Africa, now called Heart for Africa. I knew this was an answer to my prayer and an opportunity to help and make a difference where I dreamed of for so many years.

Soon I was jetting off to Swaziland, a small kingdom in Sub-Saharan Africa. It's the No. 1 HIV/AIDS-infected country in the world. Forty-four percent of the population is infected, and consequently there are more orphan-headed households per capita than any other country. The tiny nation, about the size of Hawai'i in people, was dying. There are more deaths than there are births.

After a 19-hour flight from Washington, D.C., to Johannesburg, South Africa, our group went east by bus for about five hours into Swaziland. As soon as we got off the bus after all that traveling, our missionary leader on the ground said, "How many of you want to go to an orphanage right now?" Though exhausted, several of us said, "Yes." On the short drive, I tried to imagine what this orphanage would look like. I'd always pictured an orphanage as a building, perhaps somewhat austere, with bunk beds lined up, and certainly a big kitchen with lots of food being prepared. As we turned into a dirt drive I looked for "my orphanage." We stopped alongside a very small structure that looked like an outhouse and saw about 20 little children from ages 2 to about 7 sitting in front of it on ragged mats on the dirt. Their clothes were tattered and their faces were filthy. Nearby, under a scraggly tree, a pot of cabbage boiled on a small fire. Among the women there was an older woman, who we were told was a "GoGo," or grandmother. Four young teenagers helped out with the children as well. This orphanage started because the GoGo had collected orphans as they wandered up with nowhere else to turn. She cared for them under that tree as best she could until organizations such as ours started to help.

I soon learned that an orphanage in Africa consisted of a gogo and children, most likely orphaned because of HIV/AIDS. Often, there is no roof over their heads, only a kind-hearted soul who decided to take responsibility and care for them.

Children wander up in greater numbers all the time. They're being orphaned in Africa at the rate of one child per second. In the time that you've been reading this, how many children does that make? It's a mind-boggling challenge. That's why I'm passionate to try to help in some way. The children deserve better. They don't deserve to be discarded much like the garbage they eat at the city dumps to survive.

Often people say, "Oh, Africa has always had these problems. You can't make a difference there, so why bother?" But you bother, because isn't one child worth saving, loving and giving hope to? If you save one child or two children, or four, or five, well, doesn't that make flying halfway around the world worth it? There are many hopeful examples of children who have been saved and orphanages that have been built so that these little ones could be given a chance. There's a lot of work to do. But, as Bono said, it should be an adventure.

Whatever you decide to do, make sure you are passionate about it, something you care about that you know will make a difference. Time is of value, and oftentimes we don't have much of it because we are working and running a family at home, but we are so blessed with so much that we take advantage of daily. When things become routine and you find yourself on the same path, create an adventure, and make a difference in Africa or Hawai'i by helping those who really need you to extend your hand to them and fulfill your purpose.

*"Life is a blank page,
an unwritten song, an empty
canvas—until you begin
to write your own script,
living out the movie you create
from every day of your life.
So why not imagine
a perfect world?"*

Edgy Lee
Chief Executive Officer
FILMWORKS PACIFIC

Aloha Spirit

Mike McCartney, Chairman, Democratic Party of Hawai'i

My dad is an Irishman from Oklahoma. He moved from Council Bluffs, Iowa, to Hawai'i in 1930 to teach at Maui High School. As a 27-year-old, first-year teacher he received a bonus of $1,000 and a house. He taught Japanese, Chinese and Portuguese kids, including some notable locals, such as Leonard Rego, senators Mamuru Yamasaki and Nadao Yoshinaga, house speaker Tadao Beppu and NASA scientist Walter Higa.

During his first week of work he, along with the other teachers, were invited to the plantation manager's house. While they were eating off of the host's fine china, the plantation manager told all the teachers, "Thank you for coming to Maui. Your job is to teach them, but just remember one thing. Do not teach them too much"—because we want to keep them on the plantation.

When I turned 21, my dad gave me this great poem that he wrote. One of the lines read, "The cosmic dust that you borrow from the universe, give it back in brighter coin than you received." With that in mind, I think my dad did his best to teach the plantation kids "too much." That was his way to create balance and social justice. That was his purpose, to give people the tools to realize their ability to do more with their lives.

Now, my purpose in life is to be of service. I can help people in small ways and big ways. To me, I think our challenge in life is not to define ourselves by how much money we make or what title we hold, but rather by the things we do to make things better.

You know, we call it the "aloha spirit."

There's a lot that we can share and do. You can always be of service all the

Mike McCartney serves as chairman of the Democratic Party of Hawai'i, and is a former Hawai'i state senator. He's the former president and CEO of PBS Hawai'i. Mike was instrumental in creating and producing *Hawai'i Stars*, a forerunner to the national program *American Idol*. He served as cabinet member under Gov. Benjamin Cayetano (1999 and 2000), as the director of the state Department of Human Resources Development. He is a board member for the Hawai'i Justice Foundation, Royal State Trust and Center for Alternative Dispute Resolution. He is also a member of the Board of Trustees of Pacific University in Oregon.

time, every day, in everything you do. That's why the "Live Aloha" sticker was created with Robbie Alm, Haunani Apoliona and others. The original intention was to try to change government, but we also realized that what George Mason told us was true, "'Ey, we got to change ourselves."

Those Live Aloha stickers are really reminders that, "Hey, you can make a difference. You can return your shopping cart. You can say 'thank you' when people let you cut in. You can pick up the rubbish off the ground."

Little things like that are services and I think if we do that in our everyday lives, we are living successful lives.

I like to help people. My purpose in life is to be of service and my service is bringing people together to solve problems. Not everybody does that. Not everybody can do that, but that's my role.

What I've homed in on—or at least in my ego or my mind—is that I bring the right people together to solve problems or do special things. There are people today that are my friends, who didn't know each other before, and now they have formed companies together. Together we can make a difference. And so to me Hawai'i is about being of service.

*"What I do for a living
is not a vocation.
It's not a hobby;
it's not a passion;
it is pure and simple
—an obsession!"*

Mike Post
Owner
MIKE POST PRODUCTIONS
EMMY AWARD AND FIVE-TIME GRAMMY AWARD WINNER

2

FOLLOW
YOUR PASSION

2

FOLLOW YOUR PASSION

Evan Leong, Chief Executive Officer, Greater Good Inc.

When I was in college, my roommate and I started a clothing business. We bought a sewing machine, a serger and all the other equipment we thought we'd need. The first clothes we made actually looked pretty good. That was until we washed them. I pulled a new parka out of the dryer to find that one sleeve had shrunk by six inches while the other had stretched. The whole parka was lopsided, including the collar. Needless to say, that business quickly ended. Still, I had learned something important. I realized that I loved the thrill of launching and running my own business. I found something that I had a passion for.

When we first started on this Greater Good project of interviewing people with great success in business, we thought that their advice would be all about strategy, execution and business jargon. Boy, were we wrong! The number-one reason that they gave for their enduring success was a passion for whatever they were doing. These people were so passionate about their businesses, families, lives and communities. It was contagious!

The saying by the ancient Chinese philosopher Confucius came up over and over again: "If you're doing what you love, you'll never have to work a day in your life."

This became especially apparent in a lunch meeting I had a few years ago with Mike Post, a music industry legend. I had first met Mike at my brother's high school graduation party. It wasn't until much later that I got the opportunity to sit down with him and have an in-depth discussion. That lunch meeting changed my life.

We met to talk about marketing Hawaiian music because I was doing consulting work for a local music label. I was asking Mike for his advice because of his expertise. Mike has more than 6,000 hours of television and movie music scores produced and has at least two pieces of music playing somewhere every single minute, all of which earn him huge royalties. The amazing part is that he'll receive these royalty payments for 75 years after he's dead! I went to talk business, but what I got was something entirely different.

Mike's passion seeps out of every pore in his body. He eats, breathes and sleeps music. He writes music every day. He even invests in music projects with a high chance of failure just because he loves music. The key is that he found a niche to turn his passion into a very lucrative business and profession.

Mike was 60 years old at the time of our lunch meeting. When it was over, it occurred to me that if I could have just 10 percent of the passion for what I do as he had, my life would surpass my expectations. Such passion becomes the emotional fuel to overcome obstacles, failure and negativity. It's the fuel needed for enduring success.

Jim Collins wrote a national best-seller called *Good to Great*, in which he advises us to first ask "who" and then ask "what." First find the right people and then determine your business strategy.

But in our research for this book, we found that even before we ask "who" we need to ask another question: first ask "why" and then ask "who."

The "why" will lead us to our passion and will then help determine the "who." Asking why allows us to take a step back and look deeper into what really makes us passionate. Here are a few questions to help with this:

Why am I doing what I'm doing?

Will it make me happy and fulfilled?

Will it lead me closer to my purpose?

Will I be able to make a difference?

If today were my last day on earth, am I doing what I'm passionate about?

These questions are the same ones I ask myself on a regular basis. They have changed the way I look at things. They have changed the way I evaluate opportunities and endeavors. Asking these questions allows me to find the emotional fuel I need to keep on keeping on.

Passion can be fueled by negative emotions like anger, jealousy and greed, but in my own life I find the energy to be much more stable when fueled by the path to my purpose. You can tell when people are fueled by passion. They walk differently. They talk and look different. They also get different results.

My wish for you is that, if you haven't already done so, find your passion and then pursue it with all you have. Here are some stories from those who have found their passion and the results they have enjoyed.

*"Being involved
in a near–death accident
really puts things
in perspective pretty quickly:
Life is very, very precious
and I better do something really big.
I've been given an opportunity
to make my mark and
help other people."*

Shelley Wilson
President
WILSON HOMECARE

It's an Obsession

Mike Post, Owner, Mike Post Productions

My goal was simple: Make an honorable living doing music. When I was 18, making music to me meant playing in a band or being a studio musician. If that didn't work out, I'd play a gig at night or teach kids during the day. And if that didn't work out, I'd play an organ at a funeral home—that would have been fine. I just wanted to make an honorable living doing music.

While I was trying to realize that dream, I got very fortunate. Actually, I was lucky from the beginning because I was born with some natural talent. I was also fortunate because my parents made me believe I could do anything that I wanted to do; anything that I could conceive. They made me believe that I was smart and disciplined enough to figure out a way to accomplish it.

The truth is that what I do for a living is not a vocation. It's not a hobby. It's not a passion. It is pure and simple—an obsession.

Now, when I speak at colleges like the music class at the University of Southern California, a student usually raises a hand and asks, "Why did you get into this?"

I answer, "Ask the kid sitting next to you because they probably know. In fact, three-quarters of you guys in this class probably know."

And somebody always raises a hand to volunteer the answer.

I say, "OK. Tell him."

And the student explains, "It's because you had no choice."

"Right," I say. "That's exactly right. No choice."

It defines who I am. That's me. I think first I'm a human being. Second

Mike Post is owner of Mike Post Productions. He won his first Grammy Award at age 23 for Best Instrumental Arrangement on Mason Williams' "Classical Gas." Mike has won five Grammy Awards, an Emmy Award and a BMI Lifetime Achievement Award as a music producer. Mike has two pieces of music playing every minute. Starting his music career in the 1970s, Mike has written more than 6,000 hours' worth of music for film and television, making him the most successful composer in the industry. He has produced the signature melodies for programs, such as *Magnum P.I.*, *NYPD Blue*, and *Law & Order*. Mike also produced the first three albums for Kenny Roger's country/rock group The First Edition along with Dolly Parton's hit album *9 to 5* and *Odd Jobs*.

I'm an American and third I'm a musician. I've been doing this since I was 6 years old. There's no choice. It's just what I do.

If they didn't pay me to make music, I'd do something else to support my family and I'd do it at night. I'd still be a musician. But the truth is that it's not a choice, absolutely not a choice.

Am I a pilot? Yeah.

Do I fly my airplane? Yeah.

Have I learned a couple other things? Yeah, but I'm in mono. I'm one thing.

*"You need some other thing
besides work
that you care about,
that you love doing."*

Don Chapman
Editor
M*ID*W*EEK* **AND** *HI* L*UXURY*

Crazy to Visionary

Darren T. Kimura, Chairman, President and Chief Executive Officer, Sopogy, Inc.

When I was a child growing up in Hilo, Hawai'i, I had dreams of becoming a big-time business leader. When I graduated from Waiākea High School in 1992, I left Hilo to attend the University of Hawai'i at Mānoa to begin that process. I thought I'd learn more about business by doing, rather than by sitting in a classroom, so I took on three jobs. My first job was selling power tools, the second was selling women's shoes and the third, working at the University computer lab.

While I worked a lot, I also surfed a lot. It was a hobby I picked up in high school and was important to my lifestyle and image. I tried to look and act the part of a surfer, so I was extremely suntanned and had bleached hair. Nearly every other word I used was in pidgin, I wore a Hawaiian fish hook pendant around my neck, and, of course, I wore multiple earrings on each ear, which was popular at the time.

By my sophomore year of college, I felt I was ready to try my hand in business. My father, who owned an electrical contracting business, saw that there was a need for alternative energy. He proposed joining his company and growing a new energy division. Based on his advice and after some research, I decided to pursue this but do so in my own company. I quit my tool job and my computer lab job and started Energy Conservation Hawai'i, the first building block of Energy Industries. My goal was to help people save money by saving energy. At the time, the concept of energy conservation was extremely unpopular in Hawai'i and insiders told me that I was absolutely "crazy" to pursue it. It was crazy to challenge the electric utilities, crazy to

Darren T. Kimura is the CEO and Chairman of the Board of Director for Energy Industries Holdings, Inc., a global conglomerate of energy companies. His nationally recognized businesses include Energy Industries, Sopogy, Energy Laboratories, and Oasis Innovation. Darren has been recognized as the Ernst & Young Emerging Entrepreneur of the Year, SBA Young Entrepreneur of the Year, Sustainable Entrepreneur of the Year and Energy Pioneer of the Year. He is also a recognized expert, speaker and writer in the field of energy efficiency and renewable energy. Darren is proud to be an Eagle Scout and has a Bachelor of Arts degree from the University of Hawai'i and a Bachelor of Science degree from Portland State University.

endorse new, unproven technologies in Hawai'i, global warming was fiction so I was crazy to talk about it and I was crazy to pass up an opportunity to take over a successful family business. My first year proved the insiders right. The business wasn't successful, and selling shoes kept me alive while surfing kept me sane. After a year of door-to-door sales to small businesses, I realized it was taking as much time to sell a small job as it would a big job. I thought a bank would be the lucky big job that could make my business an overnight hit.

I was persistent in making calls to different financial institutions and strategic in my approach. After a month, I finally got a bank president to schedule time to listen to my pitch. After catching a few waves at Ala Moana Beach, I headed to my meeting.

In a come-as-you-are kind of appearance, I began my pitch. After only 10 minutes into my 30-minute presentation, the president stopped me dead in my tracks and literally kicked me out. But not before sharing a few words with me. In that short period of time, I was shattered and my confidence and self-worth was gone.

I left that meeting completely torn up. I was in tears and my spirit was crushed. Because this was a dream from childhood, the rejection hurt even more knowing I was on a path where my goals were unattainable. I wanted to give up on everything.

A week passed and I needed closure. I called the bank president, several times, and on a lucky attempt, caught her. Before she could hang up, I begged her to tell me what I did wrong. She agreed and was completely forthcoming. She said I showed up late, spoke too fast, used too much pidgin, dressed poorly, broke all the polite rules of business, looked terrible and smelled even worse. It demonstrated a lack of respect for the bank and for her. I took it all in and when she was done, begged her to give me one more meeting. She agreed to see me again in two weeks for a 10-minute meeting.

I knew I could do better than that first pitch. I realized my dream was still alive and was more important than preserving my surfer image. I cut my hair, ironed my clothes, lost the earrings, dumped the pidgin and practiced my pitch to anyone who would listen.

On the day of the meeting, I showed up early and was prepared. Originally scheduled for 10 minutes, the meeting continued for an hour, after which I walked out with a signed contract. I was a completely new person, inside and out.

This event marked a turning point in my career from being an irresponsible surfer to professional businessperson.

Today, with oil prices and energy costs at all-time highs, global warming on the top of mind and sustainability a primary issue, people tell me I'm a "visionary" to be in this industry. As I look back, I reflect on my perspective and how I went from "crazy" to "visionary" in just a few years. In a matter of minutes, my perspective on self-worth changed. In a few hours, my perspective on my dreams changed. In a matter of days, my perspective on the path I needed to pursue changed. And it came down to one person and a few minutes of keeping it real, to put me on the right path. Following your dream, even in your darkest hour, is my secret to success.

*"Everybody is busy in
the current day and age,
but pick something
you really believe in,
that you're passionate about,
and get involved."*

Admiral Thomas B. Fargo (USN Ret.)
(Former Commander, U.S. Pacific Command)
President
TREX ENTERPRISES

Find Your Passion

Crystal Rose, Partner, Bays, Deaver, Lung, Rose & Holma

Hawai'i is a special place that we all call home. I always knew I wanted to come home and raise my family here. It's a wonderful place for children, it's a wonderful place for family. It combines family, community and business in a way that I don't think I've ever seen in any other city in the world. I have a passion for Hawai'i, for its people, for its land and for its culture.

So I always say to young people today, "Find your passion." When you find your passion, then work is easy, it's fun and you'll want to give back to the community. With that, only good things can happen. Passion is not something you'll find on a SAT test, or an LSAT or anything like that. It's inside of you; it's what you care deeply about. It touches your heart, your soul. It drives you when nothing else can. It drives you when you're faced with opposition but you truly believe in what you're doing and why you're doing it. It's what makes people do the extraordinary!

I have a passion for helping people solve their business problems. And for making our Island home the best it can be. As lawyers, we shouldn't create problems. People hire attorneys because they have a problem they can't solve by themselves. My job is to find creative, strategic solutions to complex business issues that work for everyone.

I am also very passionate about our Native Hawaiian community. It defines who we are as a people and as a community. Hawai'i is a special place because of its people, its culture and its sense of place. As a privileged beneficiary of the

Crystal Rose is a partner at Bays, Deaver, Lung, Rose & Holma, specializing in commercial, real estate, construction and trust litigation. Crystal started her career as an associate at Carlsmith Ball and taught construction law as a lecturer at the University of Hawai'i from 1986 to 1989. She sits on the board of several organizations, including the Central Pacific Financial Corp.; Central Pacific Bank; Hawaiian Airlines; Gentry Homes, Ltd; Boys & Girls Club of Hawai'i; Friends of 'Iolani Palace and Native Hawaiian Legal Corporation. Crystal sat as commissioner of the Ethics Commission of the City & County of Honolulu in 1986. In 2000, Crystal received the O'o Award, Hawaiian Business Person of the Year, and in 2005, the Pacific Business News Business Woman of the Year Award, for her outstanding performance as an entrepreneur and community leader.

Kamehameha Schools, I recognize my responsibility to servant leadership. We all need to do our part to take special care of each other, to protect our host culture and to make this place we call home, the best that it can be. My community involvement is my way of giving back. In my eyes, it's not community versus business. It's all one. What's good for the community is good for business. Getting involved in the community offers new and different perspectives. It develops leaders. It teaches lessons and gives experiences that aren't available in business, but in the end, it enhances your business. They complement each other. It all works together. You meet people, you meet clients. My best clients are my friends and I've met them in the community. I tell all of our young associates in our office, "Find something that you're passionate about and get involved in it."

My sons are teenagers in high school. My husband and I constantly say: "Find something that you truly want to do and go do it! We'll support anything you are passionate about!" Hopefully, they will find something that will touch their hearts and make them want to give back to the community in a way that's important.

Find your passion.

*"Look into your heart
and take on the cause
that you are really, deeply
passionate about.
If you are deeply
passionate about it,
the cause will take you over."*

Mitch D'Olier
President and Chief Executive Officer
**KĀNEʻOHE RANCH COMPANY, LLC
AND HAROLD K.L. CASTLE FOUNDATION**

Double Lifers

David Heenan, Trustee, Estate of James Campbell

What does it take to mold a double life? For starters, it requires tremendous drive and confidence to jettison a conventional lifestyle and head into uncharted waters. People seeking two challenges are highly motivated.

With a degree from Boston's Berklee College of Music, stockbroker-musician Doug Lees felt a void in his Wall Street career until he formed his rock band, The Wingnuts. "I didn't know why business success was not as fulfilling to me as it was to other people," he said. "The dreams of your youth are so strong that if you try to deny them or leave them for too long, you could end up in psychic peril." But his return to the keyboard changed all that.

That kind of spunk pays off. Those contemplating a second life are undaunted risk takers. Harvard-trained Ethan Canin had the grit to leave the medical profession after only seven years. At the time, he confessed: "It makes me understand that it's the idea of writing a great book that propels me now, whereas it used to be the idea of success." Redefining success on his own terms had an immediate effect on the now highly acclaimed author: "I remember the morning of walking out of the hospital and into this shining day and just feeling this flood of relief."

Curiosity is almost as important an attribute as grit. Art historian Kenneth Clark called Leonardo da Vinci "undoubtedly the most curious man who ever lived." Today, doctor-inventor Harry Gruber rages with the same unbridled curiosity. At age 27, he secured his first patent for a class of compounds that regulate andenosine, a building block of DNA. Now 58, the biotech expert and serial entrepreneur founded the San Diego-based Kintera, Inc., an Internet marketing provider for nonprofit organizations. "Harry has an amazing range. His mind is like a Web page with about 62 links," says J. William Grimes, a longtime colleague and former chief executive of ESPN.

Besides being hyperkinetic, these people have a well-developed ability to concentrate while leading two lives. Poet-pediatrician William Carlos Williams wrote in his car while parked outside patients' homes after he made his house calls. With more than 14 million books in print, David Baldacci also knows how to focus. Cranking out a thriller a year, the lawyer-turned-writer says he "zones out a lot." "I can write with a crying child on my lap," he said. "I have, often."

Many people launch a double life from their day jobs—which can benefit the employer as much as the employee. In our "innovative economy," talent is what matters most, and smart leaders help create a corporate culture that unleashes, not stifles, human creativity. Savvy organizations, such as Microsoft, General Electric and Cisco Systems, recognize that a serious avocation can enable people to escape creeping corporate boredom.

For years, Sony's former chairman and chief executive officer, Norio Ohga, had a rich life outside the company as a jet pilot, an operatic tenor and an orchestra conductor. Instead of haunting Sony's offices in Tokyo, he chose to fly around the world pursuing his musical interests. Not your average salary man, this managerial maestro tapped his baton in leading symphonies on almost every continent and chaired the Tokyo Philharmonic. Whether in business or in concert, Ohga convinced his players that they were free to express themselves, while still getting them to follow his vision and direction. When he assumed the top slot at Sony, Ohga brought not just demonstrated talent and experience, but a ton of less obvious assets, such as self-awareness and independence, that served both him and the company. That kind of self-esteem guarantees outstanding leadership.

Of course, not everyone is meant to have a second life. What's an escape route for some can be a bumpy road for others. Not everyone has the natural ability, independent of drive and intelligence, to act, write, paint or launch a new venture. An inborn knack for storytelling, a good ear for music, a good eye for the visual arts, a flair for entrepreneurship—these gifts are unevenly distributed. So wannabe double lifers have to get real in assessing their strengths and weaknesses.

The wise person defines success not in terms of being famous, but in terms of happiness and personal fulfillment. To accept any other definition is to lose the control we have over our destinies. You can't necessarily make yourself into the next Leonardo da Vinci. But you can convert your talents into a craft that can be practiced in hundreds of ways, from painting to public speaking. If, in the end, you become as rich and famous as Norio Ohga or Michael Crichton, so be it. But even if you reach modest heights, you have found a way to live well.

*"Live life like
a cherry blossom.
They're glorious and
they stay open for only
a week or two.
Be in your full glory
all the time by giving
your best all the time
and achieving
your full potential."*

Sanford Murata
President
SANFORD MURATA, INC.

Lifelong Coach

Rick Blangiardi, President and General Manager, KGMB9 Television

Passion. It is such a strong word. I have a passion for people and I look for that same quality in others. Despite my role in a job, I'm probably more passionate about the people I'm around than the work itself. One of the roles I played in my lifetime was as the head defense football coach for the University of Hawai'i. There was one "passionate" game that I'll never forget. I remember the day clearly …

It was opening day at Washington's Husky Stadium before it was expanded, but it was still an incredibly large stadium. The UH Rainbows vs. Washington Huskies game was supposed to be just an opening day event for the team that was heading to the Rose Bowl. The stadium was packed, Lake Washington was lined with spectators' boats and it was a beautiful, sunshiney day. Just prior to leaving the hotel, I remember watching TV and there was a guy named "Jimmy the Greek" talking about the game. In 1973, he was well known for predicting the outcome of the day's games. That morning he said, "Out in the far west and a real tune up for the Huskies, it will probably be a real good laugh when the Huskies play these guys from Hawai'i …" something along those lines. "The Huskies will win by 50 plus," he predicted.

We were facing a very hostile setting. We were incredible underdogs, but we were going against a very formidable opponent that was stacked with talent. Under those circumstances, it seemed almost impossible to win. Regardless, we were on a mission. We were representing the state of Hawai'i, including all of the UH fans who came out to support us.

Rick Blangiardi is the president and general manager of the Hawai'i CBS affiliate KGMB9. He started his media career as an account executive for KGMB9 in 1977. Five years later, Rick moved up the ranks to become general sales manager. From then on he worked for several media companies in Hawai'i and the Mainland. Prior to his professional media career, Rick was an assistant coach for the University of Hawai'i's football team, eventually becoming associate head coach and defensive coordinator from 1975 to 1977. In 1970, he was honorably discharged from the U.S. Naval Reserve. Rick is on the board of Honolulu Boys Choir, Aloha Council Boy Scouts, Chamber of Commerce, Aloha United Way and Hawai'i Food Bank.

As coaches, we never went into a game telling our players, "Let's just go out there and play respectably." Instead, we told the kids, "Hey, what you give out there tonight is what you're gonna keep and what you save will be what you lose. It is about giving it, giving it all." We told them, "We're gonna win and this is how we're gonna do it."

Rallying the team was always part of the fun of coaching. It's the origins of selling. It's selling the game plan to your players; then, as a team you're convinced that you are going to win. UH had really physical guys, so the team's head coach, Larry Price, used the expression, "Physical superiority cancels out all theory." At the time, we were 9 and 2—we had the talent, we had the theory and we had the physical superiority—we just weren't sure if it was enough.

The game opened up and the Bows scored first. Then the Huskies tied it up and continued knocking on our door. In the second half alone, there were four goal line stands. Washington was just so arrogant and determined that they would just run over us. As the coaches watched the game from the sidelines, we kept asking, "Can our guys hold on? Can they hold on?" In the course of the tough game, we anticipated that our players might give in and punch out. They never did. They couldn't, they wouldn't.

Besides holding Washington at the goal line multiple times, the UH kicker, Reinhold Stuprich, kicked a field goal to win it for the Bows. It was an incredible game.

That night, the game balls were given to the coaches. After the celebrations resided, I couldn't go to sleep. I kept thinking about the game and the kids. I decided to cut up my game ball and give every defensive player a piece. On one side I wrote, "Hawai'i 10, Washington 7. September 15, 1973." I actually carried my piece in my wallet for 20 years or more. It reminded me of the passion we all shared on that special day—to be our best, give it our all and win.

I retired from coaching some years ago, but I will never forget how proud I felt that day, in that moment. It was one of those experiences that will last way beyond a Saturday afternoon.

My passion for the people of Hawai'i, and the place itself, will forever be close to my heart. From the first day I arrived here with my parents, I loved this place. Sometimes I have to pinch myself to remind myself of the beautiful place I live in, and of its incredible people. One can easily get caught up with demanding workdays, because you love what you do. But it's important to appreciate and love Hawai'i and the people who make it unique. Passion for the Islands' people opens your eyes to everyone's talents and contribution to the community. Sustaining aloha makes Hawai'i a better place for locals and tourists, and will be an invitation for future generations to make memories here, too.

*"You need to do
what you love
and love what you do
to be successful."*

Darren T. Kimura
Chairman, President and Chief Executive Officer
SOPOGY, INC.

Passion and Hard Work

John Bower, Co-Founder and Managing Partner, Sennet Capital

Passion plays a huge role in my life. I'm passionate about my family and I've always been passionate about business. As a teenager, I ran small businesses and experienced the upside of being my own boss. The entrepreneur bug bit me.

My dad was the swimming coach for Tulane University in New Orleans, LA. My father's swim teams were undefeated for a dozen years. When I was 13, I followed my father's footsteps and combined my passion for swimming with my love for business. I worked summers teaching swimming lessons in small neighboring towns. Since my family's name carried a lot of weight in the southeast, "swimming families" offered me a place to live and a car for the summer. Over the years, my summer business adventures helped pay for my education at Cornell University.

I tell my children all the time to find their passion. I urge them to get in touch with what makes them happy. If they can find a passion, my wife and I want to support them in it, whether it's a passion for sports, music or education.

Secondly, I teach my kids that they have to work really hard at whatever it is they choose to pursue. Nothing that comes easily is as rewarding as something for which you had to work. We try to show them that without hard work, they won't feel fulfilled by their success.

For example, I asked my son, "If you could do anything, what would you do?"

He answered that he wanted to magically dunk a basketball.

"If you could dunk a basketball without even needing to try, then you wouldn't feel the thrill that you might expect," I explained to him. "On the other hand, if you worked on the dunk

John Bower, co-founder and managing partner for Sennet Capital, has 20 years of business experience managing high-growth companies. Prior to Sennet Capital, he served as the CFO and COO at Hawai'i Biotech, where he helped to secure more than $50 million in equity and grant funding. He co-founded and operated HealthRev, a national healthcare front office outsourcing company in Chicago. In less than three years, John expanded HealthRev to 10 states, with more than 200 employees and $5 million in annual cash flow. He serves on the boards of several Hawai'i and Mainland companies, including the Gift Foundation of Hawai'i.

for years until you finally got it right, the feeling would be so much more rewarding because it was a great personal accomplishment."

Thirdly, I encourage my children to maintain a balanced life. Everything that they decide to do, they must invest enough time and energy into each of their roles, whether it's student, worker, son or brother.

I was lucky enough to find my passion early on. Being a businessman and helping large and small businesses grow into successful companies has been a lot of hard work. Regardless, I love the pressure, intensity and the growth in the end. It's rewarding to leave something functioning better than when you first became a part of it. Plus, I continue to make time for the things in life that are important to me, including my family. It keeps me grounded and balanced so that I continue doing what I love to do every day.

*"You feel connected when
you do something that's
meaningful and that makes
a difference, especially when
you can do it in such a way
that you're not giving a handout
to someone but rather giving
a hand up. You end up learning
as much from those you help
as the other way around."*

Terry George
Vice-President and Executive Director
HAROLD K.L. CASTLE FOUNDATION

3

GIVING BACK

3

GIVING BACK

Evan Leong, Chief Executive Officer, Greater Good Inc.

In 2002, I was having dinner at my parents' home during the holiday season and our extended family members were catching up with each other. My Uncle Chris asked me about our first business and I shared with him that it was going great because of the lifestyle it provided for my family and myself. In hindsight, I was kind of bragging about how our company was succeeding. Uncle Chris looked at me and said, "It's great that your business is doing well, Evan, but I need to ask you: What are you doing for anyone besides yourself?"

I tried to come up with a good answer, but beyond that which directly benefited me or my family, and the occasional charitable donation, I couldn't think of anything. Sometimes, the right question, at the right time, from the right person can have a huge impact, provoking thoughts of question.

My earliest memories of community service are not positive. That's because when I was young, community service for me was usually a form of detention or some other punishment. I had to do it because I misbehaved or broke the rules at school. It wasn't until many years later that I really understood the importance of giving back and getting involved in the community. Not just as a responsibility but also as a way of increasing my business and personal development.

My journey on this path was more or less serendipitous. In 2001 Kari and I started our first business importing a Taiwanese drink product called bubble tea. We achieved major growth, and our distribution soon spread throughout Hawai'i and to North America, Guam and Saipan. We structured the company so that it allowed us income and incredible flexibility. By 2003, I was 30 years old and thought I had it all. I had a successful business and my wife had just given birth to our first son.

I was even able to find time to coach girls' pole vaulting at my high school alma mater. That was where I met a very influential businessman named Duane Kurisu. I learned that Duane was owner and part-owner of many diverse businesses, including the San Francisco

Giants, the *Honolulu Star-Bulletin*, Aloha Airlines, shopping centers and other real estate holdings, numerous magazines, a radio station … the list went on and on. What's more impressive is that he was raised on a plantation on the Big Island of Hawai'i, not with a silver spoon. Duane was the classic self-made man. After I met him at a school event, I was very excited to set a meeting with him to learn how to make more money and become more "successful." At that point in my life, that was my main concern.

The meeting began really well. He told me how he got started in business and was putting together multi-million-dollar real estate deals by the time he was in his late twenties. We talked about our companies and other business ideas. Then he shared two secrets with me that I will now share with you.

"The first secret," he said, "is leverage."

We'd been discussing scholarships, so he used them as an example. "I have a non-profit foundation that helps student athletes obtain college scholarships," he told me. "I pay for the foundation's staff positions and cover the other overhead expenses. The staff contacts universities all over the country to try to get full-ride scholarships for local student-athletes. The strategy is to get three universities to compete for a student-athlete and then negotiate a scholarship ranging between $100,000 and $160,000 to cover tuition and expenses. The hard cost to get a student-athlete a full ride averages $5,000. So for every $5,000 I invest in the foundation, a student-athlete can receive more than $100,000 in scholarship money. With just a few thousand dollars per month, I can use leverage and turn it into 20 to 30 times more than that in value."

I believe that year, Duane's foundation helped line up more than $5 million in scholarships. Wow, leverage was great! I was soaking this stuff up! I was really excited to hear the next secret. Are you ready?

"The second secret," he told me, "is that I won't invest in any business venture unless it helps the community."

As I sat there waiting for the "real" secret, he said it again: "The second secret is that I won't invest in any business venture unless it helps the community."

I was confused. "But I thought I get rich now and then give back when I get older?"

"That's what most people think," he said, "make money now and then give back later. But what if there is no later? I've been successful because I gave back first through my businesses and then the wealth followed."

I was stunned, to say the least. I had thought that business was all about conquering, strategy and execution, and that your community involvement was something done separately.

This was definitely a new concept for me. He explained that it was truly helping the community that had really made him a success. This is something that I've been thinking about ever since that day. How can I make a difference, help the community and tie it into business? And that's how my new career path began.

I realized that if businesses can partner with non-profits, government or community organizations in a way that benefits their bottom-line profits, everyone would gain. Then bring in media support to promote these relationships and the people behind them. The media would add the leverage for the ideas and the growth of this synergistic approach.

It seemed like a winning formula. With everyone helping each other, it could become a self-sustaining cycle that created a competitive advantage for Hawai'i that would be extremely hard to duplicate elsewhere.

I was completing my Executive MBA at the University of Hawai'i at the time, so I pitched the idea in Entrepreneurship class. My friend Lance countered that there was no obvious gain for the media to promote this. I thought about that and replied that the media gains because the community gains, and if their advertisers adopted this mindset, it would be in their best interests to support them. I spoke to a few media companies and they told me no one would be interested. "It's not news," they said. But that didn't sit well with me, so I thought of another idea. My wife and I would start another company and actually become the media. We wrote the business plan in May 2005 with the help of some friends.

Greater Good Radio became a joint effort to use leverage to help businesses help the community in ways that also benefit their bottom-line profits. This is what is called social entrepreneurship, or dual bottom lines. How does this leverage actually work? We interview the top business and community leaders on the air to find out how they became successful. We also discuss how their community involvement has been critical to their success. By recording these interviews, archiving them and making them available through radio, TV, print, the Internet, books and events, we can carry their message to thousands and maybe millions of people. Now these business leaders can mentor people at a ratio of one to many instead of one to one. That in turn inspires new leaders and the cycle continues. We help develop people's business and entrepreneurial careers and implant a social message and a call to action at the same time. We grow socially conscious business leaders. It is very, very exciting.

What's more exciting is to see the mission actually work. Our Web site, GreaterGoodRadio.com, has hosted visitors from over 100 countries and counting. The feedback we have received has been even more rewarding.

For example, Arizona entrepreneur Joe Higgins wrote:

"I especially like the aspect of each show when the guest is asked to explain their charitable role in the communities. From listening, we've implemented a community-giving program based on some of the ideas Evan and Kari's guests shared. As the owner of a hair salon chain with 9 locations and 50-plus employees we had an opportunity to make an impact on our communities less fortunate. Using some of the ideas I learned from the show we created a program that any of our employees could suggest a charity or fundraising event and we would support their efforts. One of our employees had a relationship with a woman's shelter and we closed the shops one day and held a day of beauty for the residents. Another employee wanted to raise money for a local neighborhood center for Christmas so we held our First Annual Sports Buzz 5K Santa Run this past December. I think it's important for businesses to support their local charities. Greater Good showed me that I have an obligation to do so and gave me the tools to implement a successful program in my local market."

Greater Good TV was launched on January 20, 2007, on the Hawai'i CBS network affiliate KGMB9. The growth has been nothing short of amazing, and I honestly believe that our mission is the driver.

The purpose of this chapter is to inspire you to identify where you can make a difference by giving back. It's an opportunity to discover the aloha spirit within you and to share it with the world.

Mentoring Community

Duncan MacNaughton, Founding Partner and Chairman, The MacNaughton Group

Herb Cornuelle was a businessman and activist in Hawai'i who was involved in the development of free market think tanks during the mid-twentieth century. When I knew him, he was the successful president of the Dillingham Corporation. I worked for him, but he was also a family friend. When I was about 40 years old, he asked me to join him for lunch.

He had a talk with me that left a lasting impression.

"Duncan, for some reason your generation didn't get involved in the community in the way I think it should have; in the way my generation got involved in the community," he said.

"Help me understand with a little perspective on that," I replied. "When did you get involved?"

He said, "Well, in the corporate structure, the company's president expected, almost demanded, that his junior executives get out in the community and become actively involved in various organizations."

In fact, Herb was about 34 years old when he became chairman of the Board of Regents of the University of Hawai'i. The position was a major commitment to the community through UH. Herb politely commanded me to rally up my age group, get organized and do more.

The message was loud and clear.

As young entrepreneurs, my colleagues and I were in survival mode and were very conscious of doing things for ourselves. Unlike a corporate culture, which is more structured, we didn't feel like we had the time or the resources to throw at community work.

Following Herb's lead, I got a group of friends together and shared with them Herb's message. We were all inspired and decided to get involved in causes that interested us.

Duncan MacNaughton is the founding partner and chairman of The MacNaughton Group, which brought Costco to Hawai'i. Duncan has developed more than 1.8 million square feet of Gross Living Area (GLA) in the state in a span of eight years. In 1993, the Hawai'i Chapter of the International Council of Shopping Centers honored him as the "Shopping Center Developer of the Year." He engages in non-profit activities, serving on the Board of Trustees of Hawai'i Preparatory Academy, Punahou School, La Pietra School for Girls and The Nature Conservancy of Hawai'i.

Originally, I volunteered on the Board of Hawai'i Preparatory Academy, which was a boarding school that I had attended on the Big Island. I was very honored to be asked to be a part of that group and I gave it my all. It was very rewarding to give something back to the school that had given me so much while I grew up. I became so passionate about the difference I could make that I am still on the board to this day.

Out of that experience I realized that I am very ardent about education. I want to make a difference for tomorrow's children and give them a chance to be their best. I am now involved in two additional educational institutions. I want to give back to the schools that have provided for my brothers, sisters and sons.

So, Herb was right. His encouragement got me involved in the same community that has turned my business into a success. I also had the opportunity to be mentored by so many of Hawai'i's great leaders because they too were involved in the community.

I've learned that you can always make time for anything you want to do; it's just a matter of priorities. My perspective on work and life has changed. When I go home at the end of the day, I can now tell my wife and kids that I was not just working to make money today, but I was actually working to make a difference in our community.

*"Start where you are,
use what you have,
do what you can.
Your age doesn't matter.
It's wherever you are,
you can actually make
a difference in the community."*

Brian Schatz
Chief Executive Officer
HELPING HANDS HAWAI'I

River of Giving

Greg Kim, Founder, Vantage Counsel, LLC

In 2003 my family was getting ready for Christmas and my son, River, who was then a high school freshman, said, "Hey Dad, you know I have everything I need; don't buy me any presents. I would appreciate it if you just donate the money to the homeless."

I knew that River had a very soft heart for the homeless, but that still blew me away like it would any parent. I mean, my son is a really good kid, but even so, that was surprising.

Then a light bulb went on and I said, "Hey, River, why don't we launch a project together to raise more money than we can give?"

That holiday season, I gave him a Christmas certificate that entitled him to launch a new event, with help from his dad, that would raise money for the homeless. He came up with the idea of creating a concert that would be organized, run and performed by kids, showcasing top youth talent within the state. It would be an entertaining show, but at the same time it would help a great cause. We felt that if the kids ran the show, the community would come out big in support. River came up with the event name, Mālama Jam ... "Mālama" meaning to care for, and "Jam" to play music. The first year the Mālama Jam kids picked the Institute for Human Services as the concert's beneficiary, and raised $20,000 ($15,000 net after expenses).

The students had a terrific lineup of acts, including singers and dancers from many schools including Moanalua, HBA, Waldorf, St. Francis, Kamehameha, Assets, Iolani, Word of Life and Punahou, and received help

Greg Kim is the founder of Vantage Counsel, LLC, which is a next-generation law firm. Greg has worked with entrepreneurs, venture capitalists and venture-funded companies for more than 20 years. Vantage Counsel, a network of attorneys, concentrates on overall business success and adds value through consultation, networking and an innovative billing system that makes the most of the client's resources while increasing Vantage Counsel's profits. Greg focuses on companies that have a dual bottom line, whether it's curing cancer or solving the world's energy crisis. He was a founding director of the Entrepreneurs Foundation with former Silicon Valley Bank CEO, John Dean. The foundation helps venture-funded startups to set aside equity for future charitable causes.

from Searider Productions of Wai'anae School and from Farrington High School. Businesses provided thousands of dollars of sponsorships and people bought hundreds of tickets for various reasons—to support the kids, to help human services—but also because it was a showcase of talented youth from Hawai'i.

The kids also organized a silent auction to raise money by showcasing and selling kids' art and other donated items. Admittedly, as a startup, Mālama Jam had an unfair advantage. People can't resist helping kids, especially if they are trying to help homeless adults. That's pretty compelling. In its first three years Mālama Jam raised over $60,000 (net of expenses). After this experience I realized that kids can make a big difference, starting with an idea and ending with helping to raise thousands of dollars to touch hundreds of lives in need.

"Get involved!
The key is to start small,
but start now."

Steven Ai
President and Chief Executive Officer
CITY MILL CO., LTD.

Two Tracks to Success

Walter Dods, Chairman, BancWest Corporation and First Hawaiian Bank

I have been involved in community affairs my whole life, and I love it. Sometimes I spend 40 hours a week doing it, so it hasn't always been easy.

Walter Dods is the chairman of BancWest Corporation and First Hawaiian Bank, and is responsible for lifting the company's status to that of the largest and most profitable company in Hawai'i. Since taking over the helm of the 138-year-old bank in 1989 after the sudden death of CEO Johnny Bellinger, Walter has seen First Hawaiian's earnings rise about 34 percent to $77 million last year, while its assets have grown more than 50 percent to about $8 billion. During that period, First Hawaiian purchased First Interstate Bank of Hawai'i for $144 million in 1991, and two years later the company took over Pioneer Fed Bancorp for $87 million. The two units have since been merged into First Hawaiian Bank, which is now the state's second-largest financial institution. Walter was installed as the president of the American Bankers Association in 1996, making him the first local bank CEO to head the powerful 121-year-old trade organization. He started his career as a mail boy at what was then-called First Insurance Company of Hawai'i, Ltd.

I am not one to give advice, but I tend to get involved in things that I like. I've been involved in some art and culture organizations, but I prefer the social services side because I came up from the streets.

During my career, I worked long hours, including weekends, and got very involved in the community. Amazing things happen if you spend time in the community with pure thoughts of helping the community. Believe it or not, business benefits dramatically by it.

I tell all of our employees, if they want to make it at First Hawaiian, they have to climb up two parallel tracks at the same time—the business track and the community service track. We are not interested in people that are just one or the other. There is room for them, but if someone wants to make it to the top of the organization, they've got to go up both tracks.

I mentor and watch a lot of young execs today and what I have found is that if they only go up the company track, they just learn about their company. They don't develop a network. They don't see the greater community. They don't know what's happening.

I noticed that when they go up the community service track, because the community badly needs leadership, they eventually become a director of some organization. Maybe then they become a vice president. Before they know it, they're the president of some little community organization. Those people that go up the community service track quickly develop leadership qualities because it's much harder to motivate volunteers than it is employees.

When you get into community service, you have to lead by example and you have got to make sure the troops are following you. At the bank, the executives who take community service seriously become much better executives because they are aware of how business and community go hand in hand for success.

I sympathize with small-business people who are their own accounting departments, personnel departments, sales department, and then clean the bathrooms and everything else. So I understand it's more difficult but allocating some time—maybe 10 percent and not 50 percent—to get involved will help your business. It's an opportunity to meet a lot of people that will be lifelong friends. It just pays off and I have seen it time and time again within my own organization.

*"If we're out there
being successful, we've got to
give back to the community
that's helped make us successful.
If you see a need out there,
you've got to step in
and help solve it."*

Jeff Arce
Partner
THE MACNAUGHTON GROUP

How Do You Plan to Give Back?

Joan Bennet, President and Chief Executive Officer,
Bennet Group Strategic Communications

While I grew up in a household that was very community minded, my views about giving to others were shaped most dramatically when I was a teenager.

I went to Ghana, Africa, as part of a two-month emergency aid project with the Peace Corps when I was just 17 years old. I thought I was going to save the world. Of course, the world saved me instead! Seeing so much poverty at such a young age changed me in many ways. But most importantly I learned with great certainty that when you give to others, what you get back is always greater than what you give. Always. The Peace Corps shaped my views very early in my life about the need to give back and to help others ... if only because you gain so much in return.

When I came to Hawai'i I also got an important lesson about the need to give back, especially here in our Island community. I had been in Hawai'i for only a few weeks when a leading executive asked me out for lunch. We had not even gotten our salads when she leaned over, looking at me intently, and said, "Welcome to Hawai'i. Now, how do you plan to give back?" I was a bit surprised to say the least. After all, I had not even unpacked my things yet! But her question—and the important lesson I learned that day about what Island values we hold dear here—has stayed with me these many years.

Joan Bennet built one of Hawai'i's most successful public relations companies, Bennet Group Strategic Communications. As president and CEO, Joan led her company—Hawai'i's foremost "virtual" company—to become the fifth largest public relations firm by revenues in the state. Her company, which celebrated its 10th anniversary in 2007, provides public relations counsel to some of Hawai'i's top businesses, including Bank of Hawai'i, Maui Land & Pineapple Company, Whole Foods Market, General Growth, Outrigger Hotels & Resorts, DR Horton Schuler Division and Verizon Wireless, among others. Each year, the Bennet Group selects one deserving non-profit group and provides free public relations for 12 months. Additionally, the firm also supports other charitable organizations, including the Boys & Girls Club of Honolulu, Mothers Against Drunk Driving, Hawai'i Children's Cancer Foundation, Special Olympics and the Chinatown Revitalization Project.

Philanthropy has been an important value at my company since I started the firm a decade ago. And the importance of giving back to the community has continued to become even clearer to me over the years. Giving to others in need is such an important part of Hawai'i's culture. As one of Hawai'i's small businesses, it is both a privilege—and an obligation—to give back.

When I started my company I wanted to do many things differently ... including finding ways to use technology to allow us to work smarter and better for our clients. We were one of the first virtual companies in Hawai'i. It provides an excellent quality of life for our employees, and by keeping more cars off the road, it's great for the environment as well.

Our approach to community giving is also unique. We have made a deep commitment to giving back at our firm. Everyone is encouraged to personally get involved in whatever cause or charity they feel passionate about. In 2007, in honor of our 10th anniversary, we provided free "PR 101" workshops to more than 20 non-profit organizations working to help end homelessness and to improve public health in Hawai'i. Our goal is to build communications capacity within these organizations so that they have the tools and training they need to tell their own stories. We hope, as a result, they will be able to secure even more financial and community support for their vital work.

We all work extremely hard on behalf of our clients, so it's important to take time away from business too. I get out in nature as much as possible by biking, swimming, hiking and fishing. Whether it is hiking to the summit of Kilimanjaro or fly fishing in Mongolia, I try to have one great adventure every year. I hiked to the Mt. Everest Base Camp via Tibet last fall, and I just returned from hiking the Inca Trail to Peru. I always come back with a renewed spirit and a deep appreciation for all that we have here in Hawai'i. I always try to select travel companies that are giving back to the local community as well, so I know the money is staying in that country and helping the people there.

I think perhaps the greatest reward of doing business here is truly appreciating how Hawai'i really works.

I came from a place where it was all about individual performance. It took me a while to learn that there really is an 'ohana here, a network of relationships between people who really will do anything in the world for each other. I have come to cherish this aspect of Hawai'i and our wonderful culture here. And I feel proud to be part of that network of people who both give and receive. It really makes doing business a pleasure. It's about much more than just making money ... it's about building a better community.

When I retire someday, I hope my biggest accomplishments will be that I have lived in service toward others, whether it's giving back to the community or giving an opportunity for my employees to grow. As the next generation of leaders in our profession, I am confident they take the public-relations industry—and our community—to the next level.

*"I never serve on
charitable boards thinking
that I'll gain connections or
I'll gain some benefit for me.
Instead, I think that it's
a great organization and
I want to do as much as I can
for my community.
But as with all efforts,
lots of benefits come back to you,
and it's very nice to see that."*

Bill Richardson
Partner
**HMS Hawai'i Management Partners, Inc.
and Dragon Bridge Capital**

What Goes Around Comes Around

Paul Loo, Former Executive Director, Morgan Stanley Hawai'i

When I was looking for a house, Bishop Harry Kennedy asked me if I had any luck finding one.

"Yes, I got a really nice house on the Wai'alae Golf Course," I said. "But the trouble, Bishop, is that it's on leasehold," I added.

Harry put his arm around my shoulder and said, "Paul, in life, everything is on leasehold."

How you conduct yourself in business and how you manage your financial affairs determines many things: where your kids attend school, where you live and how you're going to retire. Many of us Hawai'i locals—second, third and fourth generations—worked our way off the plantation and into a better life. That's why I think it's *how* we build our business and spend our fortune that's important. In spite of our wealth, it's not right for us to have homes with 21-karat faucets, and his-and-hers Gulfstream V jets, which, by the way, is prevalent now. I think it's important to take the excess money, however much you define as excess, and put it toward education or charity. Help pull the next generation through the tube.

Since I retired, I have encouraged people to reexamine their trusts and wills. I ask them to see if they have any expendable money. If so, could they help others climb the wall? I enjoy doing that because I made a lot of sacrifices to get where I am today. But, I didn't become successful on my own. I did it with the help of a bunch of people who really believed in me and cared about me.

I want to spread the word that society keeps balanced by bifurcation. We have the global market making

Paul Loo was the executive director of Morgan Stanley Hawai'i prior to his retirement in early 2007. Paul was a regent of Chaminade University, and associate trustee of the University of Pennsylvania. He is one of the four founding directors of Hawai'i Pacific University, which presented him the "Fellow of the Pacific"—the institution's highest award—at its 2001 graduation. Paul was a former Director of Seabury Hall on Maui, The Church Divinity College of the Pacific in Berkeley, California, and The Clarence Ching Foundation. He passed away in June 2007, leaving a legacy in education, culture and arts in the Islands. Paul is survived by his wife, Violet, two children and five grandchildren.

enormous sums of money, but there are too many that have very little in this world. If you're making large sums of money, it is important to give other people the opportunity to grow and better themselves.

The habit of giving begins from an early age. Even if you've only got $1, try to give 5 cents. It's not the amount that matters; it is the giving process. One of the greatest fallacies in life is that "when dad leaves me the money, when my ship comes in, when I win the lottery," I'll give. Let me tell you, it never happens.

I went to school with a guy named Rodman Rockefeller, of the famous Rockefeller family. He told me that the Rockefeller kids were only given a modest allowance, and even as kids, they were told that they must donate a portion of it.

When the children grew up and become inheritors of one of the greatest fortunes in America, they knew how to handle it. This is why the Rockefellers—like Laurence who gave the entire Grand Teton National Park to charity—are so revered as a wonderful family.

I don't think that giving starts *after* you have money. I think it starts at the beginning. Whether you have a lot or a little, give what you can. There's an old passage in the Bible about someone who only gave a few pennies and actually gave more of herself than the wealthy man. Examples of helping, sacrifice and giving those in need start from the beginning.

This also applies to our businesses and employees. I've been so fortunate to have good role models whom I've worked with that showed generosity to those around them, especially their employees. I learned that we need to lead by example.

Over the years, I've had brokers who run into all kinds of trouble. One broker, for example, over-speculated and over-leveraged on a personal real estate deal—not connected with our company.

One of his apartment houses burned down and he didn't have sufficient insurance.

He was on the verge of declaring bankruptcy. He needed money so that the mortgage wouldn't be foreclosed. As his boss, I shouldn't have gotten involved with his personal business, but I loaned him the money and bailed him out.

Several years later, another firm offered him a very nice job, because he was a good broker.

He kindly turned down their offer and said, "I don't think you quite understand my relationship with Morgan Stanley."

In another instance, our Kauaʻi brokers needed help after Hurricane ʻIniki destroyed the island. They couldn't get to work. All the telephone poles were down. They had no business. Their homes were damaged.

Our office called the people on Kauaʻi and asked, "How much did you make last year?"

They told us an amount, and we said, "Well, you may not get an order for three months or more. So, we'll match what you earned last year."

"You're kidding," they said.

When another firm wanted to open on Kauaʻi and made our brokers a generous offer, they said, "No, we're not going to go out to lunch; you don't quite understand our firm."

I think what goes around, comes around. In the end, this is very valuable.

I'll give you another quick example of a secretary who worked for us. She had never been to the Mainland until she moved to California. I got her a job in our San Francisco office. One morning, she came into the office crying and smelling of smoke. Her apartment house had completely burned to the ground that night. She lost everything. Poor thing. She'd never been away from home and this was her first week.

Dean Witter came out of his office and asked, "What's all this crying going on?"

He saw this poor girl sobbing her heart out. She had come to work with the only clothes that she was able to get out with.

Dean said, "You go get an apartment. You get a new set of clothes and you send the bill to me." He added, "If you want to pay me back, you can. If you don't or you can't, forget it."

Years later, she became a vice-president of Servco Pacific, one of the largest companies in Hawaiʻi. After an earthquake in the city, she heard about how one of our employees died because his wife was trapped under a collapsed building. We got a check from this woman who said, "I haven't repaid you yet and this is my way of doing it."

When Homestead, Florida, was completely devastated, we moved all of our people into the Embassy Suites.

Our Florida manager asked, "How long do I pay the bill?"

The New York office replied, "As along as it takes to rebuild homes."

There are very few companies that will do things like that. That is the reason why I stayed around for almost half a century.

I think that we just have to remember that we're all in one 'ohana. There's nothing magical about this.

We need to lead by example. My boss, Dean Witter, was a very generous man. The company was a partnership to begin with. It was a tiny, little San Francisco firm, and all the big giants of New York snubbed us.

We didn't get any new underwritings.

One day, someone called and said, "You can be part of this underwriting in New York."

"Oh, my goodness! Thank you!" Dean reacted.

Then the underwriter said, "Oh, by the way. I went to Harvard. Would you write me a $50,000 check for my Harvard Alumni Association?"

Dean had to.

Many years later, when we were a large firm, we got the underwriting of a major west coast firm. They wanted in and Dean called up and said, "Yeah, you can come in. The University of California at Berkeley could use $50,000 for their scholarship fund. Would you send me a check?"

Dean was a very kind guy. He bailed his partners out when we couldn't sell the stock of a Bakersfield company called Kern County Land. Nobody else wanted the land, so we bought it. Dean had made a mistake. We could not sell the stock. All the partners absorbed the stock we couldn't sell. That is what underwriting is all about. Nevertheless, Dean knew that his partners didn't have as much money as he did.

He said, "Look, I'll take it off your hands."

He went to the bank and borrowed money to buy out his partners. Later, Kern County Land hit oil and it was one of the richest syndromes of oil ever found in this century. There's justice in this world. Dean became very wealthy, but it's because he respected his partners, didn't want to leave them on the hook.

Most people would've just said, "Sorry. We all agreed to go in on this. Too bad for you."

That is not the way you want to go through life. Live your life as if it is on leasehold, because at the end of the day, it is.

"I wouldn't say
giving back is important.
I would say it's a must.
I think when you reach
a certain level of leadership
in your community
as well as your career,
if you're not doing it now,
you need to."

Dennis Francis
President
HONOLULU STAR-BULLETIN AND MIDWEEK

Much Is Expected

Constance H. Lau, President and Chief Executive Officer, Hawaiian Electric Industries, Inc. and Chairman, President and Chief Executive Officer, American Savings Bank

I was fortunate to attend a school that had the motto, "To whom much is given, much is expected."

If you think about all of the people who supported you while you were growing up—your mother, father, family, friends, extended 'ohana, mentors—a lot of people cared about you. Life is about people. So I grew up with not only an expectation, but also a desire, to help other people.

One day when I was a youngster, my mom took me down to Pālama Settlement where she grew up. I thought to myself, *Why are you taking me here, Mom?*

It was a lower-income area where people hadn't had nearly the opportunities that I had growing up. As a teenage girl, visiting the settlement and hearing about my mom's childhood was probably one of the last things I wanted to do, but that experience stayed with me. My mom wanted me to know that although she and my father had done well and were able to send me to the schools of their choice for a great education, there were still a whole lot of people living in Pālama Settlement or in other "Pālama Settlements" everywhere.

I grew up with the idea that there were all these people I was supposed to help; people to whom I was somehow connected through my mom and my dad, and where all our family had come from, and that I should never forget that there were still others struggling to make a decent living for themselves and

Constance H. Lau became president & CEO of Hawaiian Electric Industries, Inc. in May 2006, which makes her one of only 20 female chief executives at the helm of a Fortune 1,000 company. *U.S. Banker Magazine* recognized Connie nationally as one of the top 25 most powerful women in banking. She has been the president and CEO of American Savings Bank since 2001, adding the chair title of American as well as Hawaiian Electric Company, Inc. in 2006. Connie was named Business Leader of the Year at the 2004 "Pacific Business News" Leadership Hawai'i event. She is actively involved in Punahou School, the Hawai'i Business Roundtable, the Hawai'i Bankers Association, the Consuelo Zobel Alger Foundation and the Maunalani Foundation, and was formerly a trustee of Kamehameha Schools.

their families. From that time on, I realized that helping out is something that all of us have a responsibility to do.

I remember early on in my career, someone told me that if I really wanted to get experience, it was easier as a woman to find it in the non-profit world. In the for-profit world, women have to make it through the ranks and get promoted to get valuable operating or line experience, whereas the non-profit world is always looking for volunteers. Thus, for any young person or woman or anyone seeking to do more in life, the non-profit world presents greater opportunity earlier in life to do important work—to run an organization, to be the treasurer, to chair the board—than you might be able to get in the for-profit world.

I've always been active in the non-profit community, and over the years it has become an elixir of sorts because volunteering and working with people turned into a wonderful thing. Especially if you find yourself in a position to make a real impact, it's ever more important to look for opportunities to help the community.

In business, we often have the resources—particularly skilled and dedicated employees—who can really make a difference in their communities if they apply their skills to non-profit work as well as their jobs. And often, it is the organizational and financial skills that business gives you that are most needed among our non-profit organizations. Getting involved is vital because if you think about all of our businesses, they are based here in our communities and on the people who live here. If you don't strengthen the community, your own business may suffer, and conversely, when our communities do well and our economy grows, we all benefit.

*"When people do volunteer,
once they start doing it,
the rest takes care of itself.
They make friends.
They get passionate about it.
They learn a lot more
about the community,
and then, usually,
it's a lifetime experience
from there."*

Gary Slovin
Managing Partner
GOODSILL ANDERSON QUINN & STIFEL

Bob's Bank

John Dean, Managing General Partner, Startup Capital Ventures

The First National Bank of Oklahoma City failed in 1986. It was the second largest bank failure in history at that time. First Interstate Bank acquired certain assets and liabilities, and it was my responsibility to go out and turn the organization around.

When I started, the bank was hemorrhaging losses. A ratio is used in banking to determine a bank's efficiency. For example, if it costs 85 cents to make dollar of revenues, the ratio is 85 percent. Banks that were run well are in the 50 to 60 percent range; banks poorly run are at 80 percent or higher. My ratio was at 115 percent. In addition, there were massive layoffs before I arrived. Most of the employees' retirement plans were in the company's stock, which was now worthless. So many employees had lost their life savings. Those who remained at the bank had also had their salaries cut. Employees were demoralized. We did a lot of things to try to improve the situation. My initial task was to spend the first two or three weeks visiting with every single employee—at every level, either in groups or one on one—and listen, listen, listen.

Early on, we brought a group of bank officers together and asked them to come up with a new set of core values for the bank. We asked them, "Apart from just making money, what do you want from this organization?" They came up with a commitment to the community, and respect and trust for employees.

Bob Huffman was one of the officers at the bank that led the core-value team. He was a natural leader and was admired and respected by everyone within the organization. The sad thing was that Bob was soon to be diagnosed with ALS, or Lou Gehrig's Disease. Within two years,

John Dean is managing partner at Startup Capital Ventures. Although John is known for rescuing financial institutions, he's most famous for turning around Silicon Valley Bank. During his eight years as CEO at Silicon Valley Bank, assets grew from $935 million to $5.5 billion; employees from 235 to more than 1,000; and market capitalization from $63 million to more than $3 billion. This was his third bank turnaround. Aptly nicknamed "bank turn-around specialist" John has established a foundation in his family name, along with an organization called the Entrepreneur's Foundation of Hawai'i, which enables companies to integrate community involvement and philanthropy into their corporate culture.

he would lose his ability to walk, then to talk and, eventually, his life.

While he fought the disease, we adopted Bob at the bank. The employees came together for him. The bank arranged a company van, with a lift in the back for his wheelchair so that he could come and go comfortably to work. Seeing Bob day in and day out was an inspiration to many of us at the bank.

If you asked me, "What does that have got to do with profitability?" I'd tell you, "Maybe nothing." But, in two years, we went from a failed institution to the most profitable bank in the state. And, I would argue that our commitment to Bob and to all employees is what drove that turnaround. The power of coming together to make a difference in the community, starting with Bob and his family, coupled with a respect for all employees, caused employees to trust again in their organization and, I believe, assisted in returning the bank to profitability.

*"I think what we want
to hear from businesses
is not only how good a job
they do, but what they do
to help grow the community
and make it a better place."*

Joan Bennet
President and Chief Executive Officer
BENNET GROUP STRATEGIC COMMUNICATIONS

*"If you think
you've got problems,
think of others.
You'll find
you're the lucky one."*

Daniel K. Inouye
Senator
UNITED STATES SENATE

4

OVERCOMING
ADVERSITY

4

OVERCOMING ADVERSITY

Evan Leong, Chief Executive Officer, Greater Good Inc.

Napoleon Hill, author of the bestselling book *Think and Grow Rich*, wrote, "Every adversity carries with it the seed of equal or greater benefit."

Jon de Mello, founder and CEO of the Mountain Apple Company, has a different twist on this:

"Every day, there are situations that you just have to tie a solution to. I've had a number of wonderful teachers but one who specifically said, 'There are no problems. They are situations that you just have to solve.'"

Jon continued to explain, "I go into life that way, into business that way. I go into it with the thought that there's got to be a solution." Jon recalls one of his teachers saying, "The solution piggy-backed on the problem."

"You always tend to look on the horizon. 'Where is the answer to my problem?' That's not the way it happens in your body, in your brain. The solution is attached right to the problem. But we tend to want to go, 'Oh, it's got to be over there. I'm going to go and poke around in that over there and see if I can find something.'"

It's not the obstacles that fill our lives that are important; it's how we deal with those obstacles. The secret to overcoming adversity is in our mindset and attitude. It reminds me of my new hobby, stand-up paddle surfing. As I paddle out on a day when the waves are a little too big for my normal comfort level, I always get a bit nervous. I look out at the waves coming in and wonder what will happen to me if I wipe out—fall off my board and get tossed around in the turbulent whitewash.

Surfing is all about commitment. When you paddle into a wave you need to commit to catching that wave. Sometimes you'll paddle hard but need to pull back for some reason. But if you start paddling and pull out at the last minute because you're scared, it starts a self-fulfilling cycle. If you do the same on the next wave and the next, it makes it very difficult to catch a single wave the rest of the day. It also shows the other surfers that you're not going to catch waves, so everyone else drops in on you regardless of what you're doing. But the reality is that it's only in one's head. Whenever I do wipe out on a wave, I always recover. It's never as bad as I thought. And I know that it's better to wipe out early and get it out of the way, because it's a rare day that you never wipe out. If I know inevitably that I'm going to fall at some point in the day, then it's better to have it happen early on.

Although it's embarrassing, I remind myself of some good advice that an experienced surfer and Waikīkī beach boy, Phillip, gave me.

He said, "Eh brah, even monkeys fall out of trees. You just get up and keep on trying until you get it."

In November 2000 my wife and I moved back to Hawai'i from California, where we first were exposed to the bubble tea drink. We had encountered an unfortunate situation on the mainland and came home somewhat broken, both spiritually and financially. But that episode hid the seed of our business to come. We started Bubble Tea Supply in 2001 with our last few thousand dollars in savings. We knew that it was a huge risk, but believed that between the two of us, it was a risk we've always wanted to take. By the end of the first year we were badly in need of money to fund our growth. We produced a retail product and launched it just in time for Christmas. Sales were booming. Our revenues had increased tenfold in the best month and we had cash flow issues just trying to keep up.

The issue with our product was that the lead time from when we ordered it to when it was delivered and available to ship was 10 to 12 weeks. This meant that in order to keep up with the projected demand, we needed to order far in advance and raise a lot more money to purchase inventory.

Since we had used the last of our money, we used our credit cards. We secured a Small Business Administration bank loan, applied for more loans and credit lines co-signed by my father, and added to the balances on numerous credit cards—all totaling in the hundreds of thousands. That was scary for us, but we needed to grow and were willing to take the risk. At that time, all we saw was growth and success in our future.

Since we had no retail distribution experience, we relied on someone whom we thought we could trust because of his retail business experience, something we lacked. This person promised us that his experience would lead us to success. He then took control of our sales forecasts, which were considerable. He would place the orders and we would pay for them.

Soon our new stock was arriving in 20- and 40-foot containers rather than pallets. We ordered hundreds of thousands of packaging bags instead of a few thousand. We used up our loans and credit cards and applied for much more capital, convinced that we were on the verge of hitting the success of early retirement.

Long story short, in January 2002 when the Christmas rush was over, our product was taken off the shelves and put in areas where it was no longer visible. We saw retail sales drop 20 percent, then 50 percent, then 80 percent, and we had to process refunds for unsold product returned to us. The man who was handling the retail distribution had the accounts with the retailers, and at one point we were owed more than $140,000. We were turned down for additional loans. In addition, we had to deal with the almost non-existent retail sales, which meant we had too much inventory and too little money once again, but this time with huge debt.

Our inventory had a shelf life, and so the retail situation grew even worse. We were forced to throw away container-loads of product and store hundreds of thousands of bags for which we had no use.

Since defaulting on the loans was not an option, we sat down and made some big changes. We also spent a lot of time in prayer. One pivotal change was to shift our strategy from retail to wholesale. The retail sales had increased the exposure of the drink, which caused an increase in demand for our wholesale customers. Another change was to make key decisions on our own; any future mistakes would be our own mistakes. We also worked very, very hard to recover from the situation.

Those decisions made a huge difference. We built a successful wholesale business, paid off the loans and, most important, gained confidence in ourselves. We focused on a national market and distribution and built strong relationships with strategic partners. Many of these relationships are stronger than ever years later. We also gained a high level of expertise in Internet technologies and outsourcing, which has proven to be priceless for our current endeavors.

Had we not gone to California and experienced that first unfortunate situation, we wouldn't have started Bubble Tea Supply. If we hadn't gone through the later challenges of our retail operation, we probably would have kept expanding in the wrong direction and gone broke. Not to mention that we wouldn't have changed our focus and learned some important lessons about faith.

I thought our own experience was tough until I met some of the people we have interviewed on Greater Good Radio and TV. Here are some of the stories they shared with us—more lessons in overcoming adversity. I hope that they will inspire you to never give up and to search for a solution when problems arise in your own life.

*"What you give
out there tonight
is what you're going to keep,
and what you save
will be what you lose.
It is about giving it your all."*

Rick Blangiardi
President and General Manager
KGMB9 TELEVISION

Bound Feet—Unbound Spirit

Vicky Cayetano, President and Chief Executive Officer, United Laundry Services, Inc.

Ah, memories of my grandmother, she was a wonderful role model for me. She had bound feet, an ancient Chinese custom where a girl's feet were mutilated and bones were broken. It was her attitude toward adversity that inspired me.

She never complained and when I would complain, whether it be about my siblings or other things, she'd say, "You know, you can always choose to say something good or say something bad, and in the breath that you have, why don't you use it to say the good?" I always remember that.

That's a wonderful memory of the influence she had on my life, how persistence and perseverance were really her mantra—especially during the World War II era. My grandfather died very young; I never knew him. He left my grandmother with 10 children to raise. With bound feet as a physical handicap and no education, you have to ask, "How did she do it?"

I'll never forget what she said when I asked her where her strength came from. She said, "You know, when I was five or six, they were binding my feet." In the process while her toes and the bones in her feet were broken she remembered saying to herself, "You can break my bones, but you cannot break my spirit."

Whenever I have challenges in my life I think of my grandmother.

Vicky Cayetano is president and CEO of United Laundry Services, Inc. and managing director of United Laundry Kona, LCC. As a former first lady of Hawai'i, Vicky is widely recognized for her many accomplishments in business, cultural preservation and promoting better health care, especially for the elderly, women and children. Her company employs more than 300 associates and provides laundry services to the hospitality and healthcare communities. When she was 3 years old, her family emigrated from the Philippines to the United States. Later, she attended Stanford University. Vicky also made a movie with Elvis Presley in 1962 titled, *It Happened at the World's Fair*. In 2000, the Girl Scouts of Hawai'i recognized Vicky Cayetano as Woman of the Year. She received the Boy Scouts of Hawai'i Distinguished Citizen of the Year in 2002, and was nominated for the Ernst & Young Entrepreneur of the Year in 1997.

*"Life is a series of
peaks and valleys.
Life is never a series
of mountaintops …
I take every experience,
positive or negative,
as an opportunity
to do better
the next time around."*

Mufi Hannemann
Mayor
CITY AND COUNTY OF HONOLULU

One Way Out

Joe Rice, President and Chief Executive Officer, Mid-Pacific Institute

I didn't have a positive outlook on life during my childhood. Looking back on it, I felt sad most of the time. The one person who kept me going was my mother, as she was the one who protected me. She took beatings from my stepdad so that I would be spared, and she hid me when she knew that he was looking for me.

She just cared for me.

I should say first off, that I'm the oldest of 12 kids. I have five half brothers and six half sisters. I'm the only one who's not a full brother. I found out later in life that I had another father. But, at the time, my mom was the only one who knew.

I was an easy target. *"You're the oldest … not my kid. Why aren't you doing your part? Why aren't you this? Why aren't you that?"*

So Mom protected me a lot. She tried her best—not always successfully.

There were a number of events that happened in my life that were key to my decision to not be anything like my stepdad. I knew that I was different, and my family always said that I was different. I didn't get drunk and I didn't react to everything with violence. I didn't go out and do questionable things, like some of our other family members. They would steal food for the family when we had nothing to eat. I would just go ask for it and see if someone would give it to us. We just had different ways of going about the same thing.

Our life was about making it through the day—whether we were hot, cold, hungry or scared. When we could, we collected things, such as beer and pop bottles, to get money to buy bread for our brothers and sisters. And a large part of the day was spent staying away from

Joe Rice has been an educator for more than 37 years with the last 11 years spent as president and CEO of Mid-Pacific Institute. Joe served four years as a special assistant to the director of education at the U.S. Trust Territories of the Pacific Islands, where he oversaw the operation of the personnel department, federal funding and grants, and teacher education activities. In 1994, Joe received the Golden Apple Award for Educational Excellence presented by Public Television and Pemco, in recognition of his passion for educating children. While in the Peace Corps, he taught high school language arts in Kabul, Afghanistan and in Saipan, Mariana Islands.

our dad to avoid getting hurt. I didn't know any other life. I thought this was it. I didn't have friends that had families any different than ours. I didn't know any better. That was the life, and I didn't see any other option for the longest time.

I remember one night my dad beat my mom up real bad, while I hid in a closet, scared. I was afraid to help her, and only later did I go to comfort her as she lay on the floor.

Since he had already hurt my mom and my sister, my younger brothers and sisters looked at me and asked, "Why didn't you help Mom? Why were you hiding in the closet?"

Earlier in the day, my dad had also hurt one of my twin sisters. Since he hurt my mom and my sister that day, I made up my mind that he was never going to do that again to any of us. I knew he would come after me so I took a butcher knife to bed for protection and I waited.

When he came looking for me at about 3 a.m., my bedroom door was locked. He knocked it off its hinges and came after me. He held the belt, the one he loved to hit us with, and swung at me while I was under the covers. I just snapped. To protect myself, I went after him with the knife, stabbing him many times. I didn't hit anything vital—though he was a bloody mess.

My family ran in and jumped him and said, "Run! Run!"

I ran away and hid in the vineyards close to where we lived for two or three days. I heard later that Dad had gone out after me with a shotgun. Finally, I got enough courage to ask for help and some people at a local convenience store called Social Services. They came and picked me up, and I was put into foster care.

My parents were barred from coming to the high school to see me, and I was able to complete high school. I worked in the strawberry fields the summer after high school and made money to buy a bus ticket from California to Washington State, and away I went.

I didn't come back to see my family for nearly seven years. I got a job in a kitchen, attended a community college and eventually graduated with a degree from the University of Washington. That was the start of my passion for helping other people, especially kids.

My adulthood began with my decision not to be a victim anymore, physically and mentally. I would not allow my stepdad to hurt me anymore. I made a decision to never get drunk, never hurt or beat a woman, and never hurt those I care about. My life would be different—it would be just the opposite. I made sure to relate well with others, to care and nurture those around me and to help those in need.

Getting into education allowed me to give others the opportunity to also make their lives better and to open doors to a better life, like the one that I was guided to.

*"My dad always
taught me to be
a big risk taker.
If you do something,
do it big
and try your best
because even if you fail
you gave it your best shot."*

Bert "BJ" Kobayashi Jr.
President and Chief Executive Officer
THE KOBAYASHI GROUP

Faces, not Butts

Richard Gushman, Chief Executive Officer, DGM Group, and
Trustee of the Estate of James Campbell

I came to Hawai'i as a merchant seaman, originally, on a research ship doing a film for *National Geographic*. We came back through here in 1971 and in 1972 I came back with my brand-new wife, who was pregnant at the time. We had our plans arranged: She was going to attend the University of Hawai'i while I was to continue my marine business.

The day after I arrived Hawai'i I was having coffee and learned while reading the newspaper that the company that was to hire me had filed for bankruptcy. Being new to the Islands and having to support my pregnant wife, I went through a career change the next day and fell back on what I knew naturally, real estate.

I remember when I was younger my father asked me every summer to go out to the field to work in construction. I remember him telling me, philosophically, all the time that it is going to be a great experience. I remember standing out there in 90-degree weather thinking this was not a great thing.

When I decided to build my own projects I recalled the experiences I had when I was younger. Those experiences and work proved to be invaluable. Like Mark Twain said, "My father got a lot smarter as I got older." I think that proved to be the case for me too.

Although I could fall back on the experiences that I had growing up, I didn't know anyone in Hawai'i. So I went around the island interviewing with people to find a job. Fortunately I was able to get several opportunities because Hawai'i was in a very strong real estate cycle at that time.

I got a job working for the McCormick Corporation, which was the largest real estate residential sales firm at the time. They had a development subsidiary that was run by a guy named Duncan MacNaughton, whom I worked for. Duncan was 28 and I was 26, and between the two of us we were very passionate about real estate.

I worked for Duncan and the company for about 11 months and I eventually decided to start my own company. This was a big risk, but I had this unshakeable confidence that kept me going, and I had the willingness to lose if that happened. I had no road map but I knew that I was willing to do whatever it took to succeed.

One of the risks I took early on was when Duncan and I decided to build Waikele Outlet shopping center.

I can't tell you how many people said to us daily, "You're going to build a 750,000 square-foot center in a sugar cane field in Waipahu?"

Many of my closest friends were kind enough not to tell me how stupid they thought the project was, but they told me afterward. We had the willingness to take a risk with the outlets and we had to have enough confidence to stand in the middle of a cane field and tell someone it would be a great place to put a big store.

Luckily, in the end, the Waikele Outlet shopping center became a success, and a lot of it had to do with luck. Luck is a huge part of everybody's journey in life. I certainly have had more than my share in that. Especially during the involuntary career shift that proved to be not as devastating as it might otherwise have been.

At the end of the day, the only ingredient that you have to fall back on is your own confidence, because at some point in every project you will come to a tipping place where it challenges your courage and sometimes you're wrong. You just have to be lucky enough or skillful enough to live through the wrong decisions, and hope that you make more right ones that are larger than the wrong ones to be able to continue at what you are trying.

It's a very destabilizing thing for high-achievement people, particularly when you think you know the answers and you've been more right than wrong. Then you have a train wreck and you have to really deal with the fact that you're neither immortal nor immune to bad decisions. You have to pick up your pieces and have the confidence and go on and make another decision, and live with it.

This happened to me when I had just finished building a large shopping center in Guam with my partner, Servco Pacific. In the course of about a 24-month period, we experienced several unforeseeable events: three hurricanes, one of which was the largest hurricane ever recorded in the Pacific; Korean Airlines crashed a jetliner into Guam, which caused a 13-percent decrease of visitors to the island; the yen went against us on a dollar conversion ratio by 40 percent; the Japanese fell into a recession; 9/11 hit the U.S. and the SARS [Severe Acute Respiratory Syndrome] outbreak in Asia stopped tourist travel.

Since we got hit with a string of events at the same time, it was really hard not to personalize one or two of them. We got pretty fatalistic about what actually was going on down there.

Although we had huge disruptions to everything, we decided to hang on. Today the project is performing really well, but it took nearly 10 years to get through it.

In a situation like this, it helps if you take care of the fundamentals. You have to have the confidence to continue and execute the plan even when it's tempting to change strategies, run in a different direction, or quit.

Walking away from it was just not an option. I think the important thing was to be religious with the routines, the disciplines and the bits and pieces that you have to do.

I think one of the tests of leadership is to be able to convince people that something is doable, even when they have great reason not to believe you.

When I was on the United Way of America's national board, the CEO of one of the big national companies told senior staff, "You know, when you're in a leadership position and you look back over your shoulder when you're out in front of everybody, you want to see faces, not butts."

If you see faces that means your people are actually following you. They're not just merely behind you. It's a huge difference.

I've had the great joy of having my son work for me, and one of the things he is learning about this business is that there comes a time in each project when the community's confidence falls away and all he is left with is his own unshakable determination. He needs the confidence that the project going to fruition will meet everyone's expectations. If you lose that confidence, it becomes contagious. It will all be gone in a heartbeat, and you can never get it back. So it's important to have the power of conviction, you have to believe it.

*"I think it's most important
to know that success
comes through hard work
and perseverance.
Never give up and if you
stay true to your beliefs,
in the end, it all works out."*

Chris Eldridge
Founder
AMERICA'S MATTRESS HAWAI'I

Confidence

Barry Weinman, Co-Founder and Managing Director, Allegis Capital

Challenges are what I think strengthen you, and I've had my share growing up.

I was arrested when I was a teenager and I thought I was going to spend the rest of my life in jail. I came from a very tough neighborhood. I have a couple of scars on my body that were pretty close to life threatening. But I worked my way out of those things.

I've got a scar on my wrist where I cut a vein in a gang fight. After the fight, my dad said to me, "You know, if you want to die at an early age, you just keep this up."

My dad struggled also because he was a baby during the Depression. During the days that he was raising me, he was going through a tough time personally, but he still encouraged me and tried to lead me in the right direction. He said, "You've got to take a whole different perspective on life. You're on the wrong path."

And it had an impact on me. I went from being a terrible student to being a pretty good student and eventually even being a very good student. I began to understand what education can do and how it can change your perspective on things.

While trying to find myself and how to change myself, my father was going through a challenging time with a business that he owned. It was in bankrupt status, but he did not declare bankruptcy. If he had, he would have been in a position where the creditors would stop coming after him.

He told me, "Although it would be easier, I'm not going to do that. It may take a long time but I will pay everyone I need to back."

We didn't have much money, but he did pay everyone he owed back. I

Barry Weinman is co-founder and managing director of Allegis Capital. Barry merged and then took his first company public, making many of his employees millionaires (including the receptionist) in the 1970s. Barry then became a venture capitalist, and he and his partners have helped over 70 companies go public. They include Palm, Cypress Semiconductor, Women.com and Medscape. With his wife, Virginia, he started the Weinman Foundation, which established the Pacific Asian Center for Entrepreneurship at the University of Hawai'i in the Shidler College of Business, and The Weinman Fellowship program for full-tuition medical scholarships at the John A. Burns School of Medicine.

learned a lot from him by just watching. At 13 years old I looked at what he did and how he kept his integrity. I said, "If he can do that under these conditions then I have to get my act together."

I learned that overcoming obstacles builds confidence. The worst thing to say is, "I don't know if it's going to work. I am scared and I don't think it will happen."

If you let that take control of you then it will be a self-fulfilling prophecy. You have to have a good level of confidence. If you believe that you can do it, even if you don't, you'll come away with lessons learned; and it will give you confidence for the next one. If you believe that you can't do it and then you don't do it, you'll go the other way because you've proven to yourself that you don't have the ability to do it.

I think what you've got to do is keep a positive outlook and say to yourself, "Look, I am putting myself at risk and I recognize that there is a probability that I may not make it. So if I don't make it, I will get back up and go after it again."

If you let something knock you down—because everybody will get knocked down at some point in time—and you don't build up a resistance to it, then you'll be knocked down forever. Instead, if you say, "Hey look, I learned a heck of a lot from this," then you are on the right track. You can't give up.

Through my career, I met a guy named Mark from Silicon Valley who had four start-up companies. He is to me the epitome of someone who has been knocked down and used it to become better. His first three businesses were miserable failures and the fourth one was sold for $14 billion. I think Mark owned around 12 percent of that company.

When people meet him, they want to talk about that one success and what he always says is, "That's irrelevant. What is relevant are the three that failed, because of what I learned, and each one of those three failures, allowed me to have the success with the fourth."

Now if he didn't have the confidence and courage to withstand the first three failures, that would be his epitaph. His gravestone would read, *Mark did these three deals and they all failed.* You have to keep trying, be confident and, most importantly, never give up, learn from the difficult times and become a better person!

"Your life doesn't define who you are. You do."

Joe Rice
President and Chief Executive Officer
Mid-Pacific Institute

Follow Your True Path

Edgy Lee, Chief Executive Officer, FilmWorks Pacific

I must have gone on hundreds of "go-sees," interviews for parts in national commercials, films and episodic TV. Some of them I got. Most of them I didn't get. At the time I was much younger and my agent was Nina Blanchard, one of the major agents in the modeling business. She signed me and that was how I made my living for the next 15 years.

But she said, "Edgy, understand that you're never going to make as much as my leggy blondes."

I'll never forget that moment.

There was nobody who looked like me, and the only other girl of color in the agency at the time was Quincy Jones' daughter, Jolie.

When I came up in front of the camera, it was a great challenge, but I soon realized that it really was not my thing. Giving all due respect to gifted actors, I began thinking that models and actors were at the bottom of the totem pole.

I wanted to write. I wanted to direct. I would read scripts and think, "Are they kidding? They actually want me to say this?"

I'd hear, "You're not Asian enough," or "We're looking for a Eurasian look with a French-Chinese accent."

I thought, "How can they spend all this money and perpetuate ridiculous stereotypes?" I always knew that I wanted more and that I could contribute more. So I moved from being in front of the camera to being behind it.

Edgy Lee is a fifth-generation Hawaii-born producer, writer and filmmaker. She is the founder and CEO of FilmWorks Pacific and the founder of the Pacific Network. Her most recent film, *The Hawaiians —Reflecting Spirit*, received rave national reviews and broadcasts on PBS. Edgy also produced two documentary films on methamphetamine in unprecedented prime time simulcasts across the state of Hawai'i. She continues to produce films on social issues. Classically trained in piano and violin, Edgy left Hawai'i to study fine arts at the San Francisco Art Institute. As an in-studio record producer, she worked with the late, famed Jamaican "Godfather of Reggae" Joe Higgs, the Wailers and other artists. She has also composed music with jazz legend Wayne Shorter and film composer, Joseph Vitarelli.

My adopted godfather was Bronislau Kaper, a remarkable man. He was from Poland and in 1935 he and his wife, Lola, fled Berlin for Paris. One evening they were down to their last few francs and Broni convinced Lola to let him take her to the poshest café in the city. In a very Errol Flynn style, Broni knew that all their money would be spent on a few glasses of wine and a shared dinner.

Sitting there, underdressed amidst high-society Paris and now penniless, Broni heard an old friend shouting from across the room, "Bronislau! A man, an American, is looking for you. He loves your music. He wants you to come and write for him. He lives in a place called Hollywood. His name is Louis B. Mayer and he's a Jew!"

Broni and Lola left for Beverly Hills, and he became an Academy Award winning composer for MGM in the days when they recorded everything live on a sound stage with 60 musicians.

His first hit song was "San Francisco" despite never having seen the city.

By the time I met him he had scored more than 150 films and was in his late 70s. I was in my 20s. He became my mentor and one of my dearest friends.

One day I told him, "Broni, I've modeled, dabbled in acting, I did children's illustration. I play piano and violin. I studied to be a serious painter and now I still don't know what I want to do. When am I going to find my niche?"

He smiled and said, "I went to law school in Warsaw because of my family. Who knew I would instead go into music? What made you think that you need to know at such a young age what you should do in life?"

"There are many doctors in your family and your parents tell you to be a doctor," he added. "So you say, 'OK, I'm going to be a doctor. Everyone in my family is in medicine and I will be happy.' Then one day you are 40 and you wake up to realize that what you really wanted to do was to be a jazz musician but you never gave yourself a chance to explore, to experience life because you were too busy studying to be a doctor. This notion of 'jack-of-all-trades, master of none' is garbage. It is a healthy thing for young people to explore life. That is what life is all about."

So who gave me the best business advice? It was Broni. He helped me realize that if I didn't have all these experiences in my life, I would not be as sensitive a director or writer. Maybe I wouldn't have been bold enough to try different avenues, including my decision to return home to Hawai'i. And I think that was a very smart decision.

When I first came home I looked for other independent producers whose goals were to produce for broad mainstream audiences. I found very few.

I came to the conclusion that in Hawai'i network television shows, such as *Hawaii 5-0* and *Magnum P.I.*, had not given "above-the-line" positions to Hawai'i professionals. No producers or writers got the kind of screen credits that allowed them to shop L.A. and bring a show back home. There were no series created by Hawai'i producers reflecting Native Hawaiians or local people in roles that were not caricatures of who we really are. So many very talented professionals went into servicing outside productions.

Instead of producing their own films or writing scripts for networks and major studios, they worked for the "other guys." Intellectual property rights were not owned by local production companies so none of that value stayed in Hawai'i, which would have inspired a real film and TV industry here.

Working on network shows is lucrative, and people have families to feed. But imagine if just one local writer had written for *Magnum P.I.* and parlayed five years of credit into a network deal. We could have seen a homegrown producer/writer create a uniquely Hawaiian series. I can guarantee you that when this happens, the content of the work will be fresh and innovative. Local people know the richness of our stories and just how deep the well is here. This is the only American community that experienced martial law in WWII. It is the only state in the union where American civilians lived under strict military rule and without their basic civil liberties for nearly four years.

This one story of ordinary people doing extraordinary acts during great adversity is one of hundreds of stories that have never been told.

When the rest of the country realizes it, I sure hope we're poised and ready. I hope we aren't sitting back grumbling and doing nothing while we watch the "other guys" come into our town to tell the stories for us. That's in part why we built Pacific Network, an Internet network of nine channels, an alternative media platform for news and original programs.

I listen to local kids and I hear a sad lack of confidence and self-assurance, which confuses me. Kids who grow up here have so much more tools than the rest of the kids in the sandbox. We understand how to get along with people from different cultures. It is an unspoken sensitivity and intelligence that is in our blood.

We all have it.

We live in the Islands in the middle of an ocean. We have limited resources and we have to sustain what we have here—culture and environment.

Being isolated is not an adversity or misfortune. It is an asset, because the rest of the world is just learning how to cope with less. The rest of the country is just now learning about cultural diversity. Families who lived on the same city block for five generations, who never had to live next to a person who didn't look like them, or who didn't eat the same kind of food, or who didn't worship at their church—welcome to the 21st century.

In overcoming adversity, I say follow your true path. Money is a necessity but when we stop chasing it, it comes. I really believe that. If you are a valet and you are happy, then that's great. If you are a lawyer and you really want to shape surfboards for a living, then do it.

Imagine a perfect world and take risks, because the alternative is not as much fun.

"*Transactional activity
generates taxable events,
but relationships build
sustainable wealth.*"

Stephen B. Metter
Chief Executive Officer
MW GROUP, LTD.

5

BUILDING RELATIONSHIPS

5

BUILDING RELATIONSHIPS

Evan Leong, Chief Executive Officer, Greater Good Inc.

I'm writing this section from a hotel room in Makati, Manila. This is my last day here, the end of a three-week trip. For the past week I've been holed up in a hotel room with two members of our Philippines team to collaborate on this book. We spent seven days and nights working on the book, stopping only for short breaks and meals.

You may ask, "How did you find people in the Philippines to work with you if you live in Hawai'i?"

The answer is simple. My childhood friend Matt went to the Philippines in 2006 to establish a branch office for the company he worked for. His wife talked with her sister, who spoke with her husband, who happened to talk to his cousin, who lived in the Philippines. The cousin is the friend of a woman who owns an accounting software business in Manila, and Matt met her through his wife's sister's husband's cousin. They now have a business handling remote workforce for foreign companies and found me two workers, Jay-R and Dan-Gil, to work with. This book was started because of their hard work and help, and it would not have been produced if Matt hadn't met his wife's sister's husband's cousin's friend in the Philippines. That is the power of relationships.

The flight between Hawai'i and the Philippines takes about 11 hours if the winds are favorable. Since I knew I'd be tired when I returned to Hawai'i, I wanted to upgrade to business class. I asked my friend in Manila if her sister—who's in the travel business—could help me with the upgrade. I thought that this would be easier than trying to call the airline myself and that maybe she could get me a deal. The result was unexpected. It turned out that my friend's sister's husband is a friend of the owner of Philippine Airlines and she was able to get me the upgrade free of charge. It's amazing what relationships can do for us.

That is the reason why I truly believe that doing business in Hawai'i is easier than anywhere else. If your intentions are good and you have the right attitude, you can meet just about anyone in Hawai'i through one or two people. The degrees of separation are much lower than in other areas and the level of trust and community is much higher.

The key component is building trust. If you look at the guest list for Greater Good Radio and TV you will find the highest level of business, government and community leaders in Hawai'i and the world. I'm often asked how we get all these busy, important people to join us on our show, especially when many of them won't talk to other media. The answer is that we concentrate on building relationships by building trust.

We started with Adam Wong, who brought the Great Harvest Bread Company to Hawai'i, because he is a personal friend and successful businessman. Since we had a relationship, we already had trust between us.

We then asked Mike Post, five-time Grammy Award-winning music producer and composer, if he would interview with us, and he agreed. Mike is a golfing buddy of my father and we had met before, so that provided the trust.

The interview with Mike made us much more confident in our ability to schedule and successfully interview high-profile people. I took the demo interview to Honolulu businessman Duane Kurisu and showed him what we had done and who was participating. I then asked him to come on the show and he agreed—after some persuasion. To my knowledge, Duane's interview on Greater Good Radio is the only long-form interview he has done.

Duane is definitely not one to blow his own horn, and people were surprised that he even participated. Nevertheless, it was a positive experience for him, and others in the business community agreed to be interviewed because one of their friends had enjoyed himself on the show and supported what we are doing.

Many of our guests don't usually talk with the media. After his interview I asked Mitch D'Olier, CEO of Kāne'ohe Ranch, if he could help us get Dick Gushman, CEO of DGM Group and a Campbell Estate trustee, on the show. Dick normally turns down interview requests from the media. Mitch called on our behalf and Dick asked me to call him before he made up his mind. He asked me about the show and I mentioned Duane Kurisu's name in my spiel. Dick said, "I'll come when Duane comes," knowing that Duane never does interviews.

I told him that Duane had already come in, along with a number of other people he knew and respected. So Dick joined us and really seemed to enjoy himself. He was also the first person interviewed when we launched Greater Good TV.

So how do we build trust with people we've never met? We always get a proper referral or word of reference. Now, there's an art to getting a good reference. The first part is to do things that are "reference worthy." People are not inclined to just refer people for no reason. The second step, of course, is to ask for the reference. If you don't ask, your chance of getting a "no" for an answer is 100 percent. The third step is not to screw it up once you get the referral. If someone refers you, they are putting their reputation on the line for you. If you disappoint the referral, you embarrass the person who referred you, and they won't do it again. If the person you were referred to is ecstatic about what you have to offer, it makes the referring party look good. In a nutshell, the person referring you has more to lose in reputation by referring a "bad egg" than by simply not doing it at all.

My philosophy is: "Treat everyone as if they are a volunteer in your organization." What this means is that if everyone were a volunteer you'd have to find ways to motivate them in different, non-monetary ways. Volunteers are much more difficult to motivate than employees because you can't use coercion. They can't be fired and you can't cut their pay, because they don't get paid. You need to find out what motivates them and treat them with appreciation and team spirit, because that's what usually drives volunteers.

Building relationships is crucial, especially in business. When times get rough or obstacles pop up, you're in for trouble if you don't have strong relationships to fall back on. Many times, in fact, it's the relationships that keep you going.

People always want to know, "What's in it for me (WIIFM)?" Knowing this, we need to concentrate on two important thoughts. The first is to always enter a relationship with a win-win attitude. Win-lose arrangements are only good for one time and will not help build a relationship. If you cut a one-sided deal, the other party still needs to follow through. Once they feel that they've "lost," they may not deliver their end of the deal. We need to cut win-win deals so that the other party really wants to deliver his or her end of the deal.

That leads to the second thought. We need to always be thinking of new ways to add value to any relationship. I believe in giving before asking. There are many ways to do this. You can help someone with an introduction or referral once you find out what they need. You can offer them free advice on subjects you would normally charge for. Most important, you can under-promise and over-deliver. This will most definitely help you build trust.

Especially because the Internet and other new technologies have leveled the playing field for business, the key differentiating factor in leadership is this ability to develop and build relationships. Many of the people we interviewed said that they determine their deals by the people involved. They decide "who" they want to work with first and then decide "what" to work on.

We've all heard the saying, "It's not what you know, it's who you know." The majority of people we interview say it's a combination of both. Here's what Hawaiian Electric Company president Mike May had to say when I asked him about becoming CEO of the largest utility company in the state.

"In the early part of your career, a lot of the critical components for success will be the technical ability to do a spreadsheet or the ability to do the quantitative analysis. Then as you move up to middle management, the mix gets richer through interpersonal skills. Then ultimately at the top, there's some component that's technical, but a big part of your job is motivational— having a vision and getting an organization to share that vision and be inspired to go accomplish it, to create shareholder value ...

People skills is not just conversation. People skills means understanding simple things like empathy. Do you have a regard for people around you? That's not conversation. That's not making small talk. Do people think you really care about them and their future?

I don't think that's introverted vs. extroverted. I think those are qualities that people can sense when you are around them, through your actions, not through your words. I think if you're true to those beliefs, I think that will come out as the leader. I can't tell you the number of times I've been looking over at my colleagues. Everything you do, from filling out an expense report to how you spend your time, you're asking people to do something that you wouldn't do. Do you model those kinds of qualities that you ask of other people? Those are the things that define a leader, not are you chatty and conversational. I didn't want to make it interpersonal as much as values. And those are important to a leader. People want a leader who can articulate a vision. But they also want to have a leader that cares about them and cares about their future."

Lastly, many people wonder how it is to work with my wife Kari. "How do you do it?" they ask.

Let me explain with a story. A friend mentioned to me that he wanted to run a business with his wife but she wasn't entrepreneurial or business minded like he was. In his mind he thought that was a weakness. I explained to him that the reason Kari and I work so well together is because we are opposites, like him and his wife. It reminds me of the story of Jack Spratt who ate no fat, whose his wife would eat no lean. I am great at starting things and Kari is great at finishing them. It almost seems as if she is good at everything that I'm not good at, and vice versa. This allows us to concentrate on our strengths while covering each other's weaknesses. We also have the same set of core values and are working toward a common goal, which allows us to work as a team instead of as individuals. We're both paddling the same canoe in the same direction, and that makes all the difference.

Relationships are key components to building a successful business and a successful life. Here are some stories that illustrate just how important this can be.

*"You will be
more successful at
building relationships
by focusing on
what you can give
vs. what you can get."*

Kari Leong
Co-Founder and President
GREATER GOOD INC.

E Puka Aku Me Kāu Mau Makana

Pono Shim, Founder, Concierge Services at Ward

For me, it's more important to build relationships and serve people than it is to earn a title. Sometimes we fool ourselves into thinking that a title gives us influence or power, but I believe the truth is that service and building relationships really create opportunities for success.

There is more to networking than meeting a lot of people or rubbing elbows with powerful CEOs.

There is a lady at Kamehameha Schools who is a caretaker for our administration. Her name is Lei. She is such a sweetheart. She does her job with so much integrity and I look forward to seeing her.

One day I saw her and greeted, "Hey, sister!"

Lei walked toward me and asked, "Where have you been?"

Then she hugged me and gave me a kiss.

She is valuable. Her well being and aloha contributes to our school and serves our community. Everybody has value, and it doesn't depend on a job title. Every personal encounter is an opportunity to build a friendship.

Pono Shim is the founder of Concierge Services at Ward. He also was the two-year president of Kamehameha Schools' Association of Teachers and Parents. With his belief in the youth of Hawai'i, he is building businesses and active in community organizations that allow children and adults to realize their potential, which is not limited by the educational and economic norms of today. Pono challenges people to compete in the fast-paced world of today, without losing their family values and integrity. His actions and beliefs have resulted in an increase in speaking engagements, requests for counsel, and mediation during tumultuous times.

I will never forget what my dad, Alvin Shim, asked me after my first day of kindergarten.

"How many friends did you make today?"

I paused, looked at him and said, "None."

"You didn't make friends today?" he replied.

"No."

"Let me teach you how to make a friend," he said. "You say, 'Hi, my name is Pono. What is your name?'"

It was one of the most precious gifts he ever gave me—the gift of invitation. I learned that a simple invitation allows people to feel that they are part of your community and involved in your life.

A sign that success has been reached is when you can leave a place in better shape than when you first found it. Success is leaving a profound and positive effect on somebody. In that way, people want you in their community. When you make a difference, people don't want you to leave. It's not because you have a title or position and they want to rub elbows with power, but because the place is better by you being there.

One way to leave a positive imprint on someone is by accepting him or her for who they are. And supporting them in knowing who they are and why they are here. By not singling out the "best" or the "most promising," you open yourself to seeing the benefits in everyone. Everyone has a gift to give, and I believe everyone has a potential promise.

The theme that comes to mind is, "Emerge with your gifts." The Hawaiian saying is "*E puka aku me kāu mau makana.*" *Makana* means your gift; *puka* means hole. "*E puka aku me kāu mau makana*" offers a vision of emerging, to break forth. Imagine a lava flow that devastates the land and covers up all the life that was once there. Then, the 'ohi'a lehua breaks through the lava. It becomes a haven and host for new life to begin again.

This image came into play a few years ago when I was on a committee that chaired the Ho'olaulea at Kamehameha Schools. The annual event is a celebration of great music, foods, fun, and service for our Kamehameha families.

The Coordinator of the Parent-Alumni Relations department each year enlists the help of parents to coordinate and volunteer for Ho'olaulea. During our first steering committee meeting I said, "I heard Merv asking for help, and too often in Hawai'i we are really good at asking people for help and when individuals come forward with their makana, their gifts, we often say, "That's great, but that's not what we need," or we say, "you have too much or not enough, or you're the wrong sex, or the wrong age," and we disqualify the gifts that are being offered and more importantly deny the heart and the spirit of possibly the person and the very thing that God wants us to have. This theme was so poignantly displayed in the movie *The Whale Rider* where the Maori clan knew they needed help and the very person who had the heart and the very gift to save her people was the very one that the chief denied. The theme of "emerge with your gifts" was not asking people to give, but rather saying, "If you would honor us with your gift, we would hold it as valuable. Nothing was too big, nothing was too small; every gift was important. Everyone was valuable."

Sometimes when committees work on these type of events, members feel like, "Oh my gosh. Let's get in and let's get out. Let's get this over with, we're done. We did our job." Instead, this committee started to have a lot of fun, and when we had challenges we'd ask, "What are we going to do?" For solutions, we turned to our theme and let it be our guide. We let the purpose be our parameter.

In February we initiated a donation day and we asked the school's families to give either flour, sugar, shoyu or rice. Socially and economically our families stretch from indigent to affluent and to ensure that every family would have the opportunity to give a donation, we asked for gifts that we felt everyone could afford.

On February 17, 2005, at 6 a.m., my job was to collect flour as the kids arrived at our elementary school. Busloads of kids from our rural communities unloaded their donations. Others drove up in cars and delivered grocery bags of flour. It was hot, fast and furious—flour bags were everywhere. At 7 a.m. the bell rang. The kids left for class, and I was stuck there with three huge piles of flour.

I started to inventory; the first pile, the second pile, and when I got to the third pile, I opened the first bag on top. And with the bag in my hand, I sat down and I began to cry. Remembering the theme, "Emerge with your gifts" and the meaning, "Nothing is too big, nothing is too small. Everything is precious. Everything is important." In the grocery bag there was a quart sandwich bag, and in the sandwich bag was a cup and a half of flour. To me, that was the most precious gift; it blew my mind that I was holding so much!

Others might look at it and ask, "Somebody gave you a cup and a half of flour?" But for me it was ho'okupu a sacred offering, and I felt that the person that gave it also offered it with five statements:

Number one, "I hear what you're saying."
Number two, "I want to believe that it's true."
Number three, "I don't have very much."
Number four, "But I'll give you everything I have."
Number five, "Please use it wisely."

I showed the donation to some of the school's leaders and an amazing thing happened. I saw people break down and cry. I saw their eyes get red and wet and nod in silent unity. I saw great people recognize the heart behind the gift and because of it stretch themselves to do more, be more and serve more.

To me, that's called raising the bar. And it is amazing to me that this generous person, that probably felt they were giving so little, will probably never know the contribution they made to so many others, especially me, and I am eternally grateful. They've built a relationship with me and relationships for me that will last a lifetime even though we've probably never met in person. They've left the community better than they found it, and that is the essence of building lifelong relationships.

*"When you're in
a leadership position
and you look back
over your shoulder
when you're out
in front of everybody,
you want to see
faces, not butts."*

Dick Gushman
Chief Executive Officer
DGM GROUP

Network for the Greater Good

Christine Camp, Chief Executive Officer, Avalon Development Corporation

There are many networking groups whose sole purpose is to meet other people. But I think the most effective kind of networking involves a common cause. That way there is an opportunity to work with like-minded people who are engaged and involved in the community. The connections made there often lead to lasting relationships.

In my case, because I joined a cause, I met people who were doers. They wanted to make a difference and that made them worth knowing. I meandered through a network of people that eventually brought me to the Chamber of Commerce of Hawai'i, where as the chairwoman of the board I had great exposure in the community. It is good not only for individual growth, but for the success of my business as well.

In 1999, I started Avalon Development Company, I joined the Chamber because I had an issue relating to my business. Due to my company's growth, I needed to hire more employees and provide healthcare and worker compensation. To control expenses, I became a vocal activist on behalf of small businesses. That pursuit led to a position on the board, and eventually I became chairwoman of the Chamber of Commerce of Hawai'i. The position at the Chamber allowed me to work with many people outside of my industry, and it helped me develop a broader reputation in the community. My good standing led to positive referrals for loans, investor offerings and new opportunities for my company.

As a member of the Chamber of Commerce, I was asked to speak at several different small-business forums. I researched all the relevant issues and reached out to labor groups, politicians, media and others to gain support for

Christine Camp, managing director of Avalon Development Company, continues to earn recognition within the real estate industry for her extensive knowledge and skilled insight into the unique Hawaiian real estate market. Christine is a real estate financial and market analyst who has built a real estate development company with more $100 million in portfolio projects under development. She sits as board member of Central Pacific Financial and vice-chairman of the loan and investment committee of Central Pacific Bank. She was on the *Honolulu Star-Bulletin* Top 10 to Watch list in 2004. In 2003, Christine was honored as Young Community Leader of the Year by the Bank of Hawai'i and, at the same year, received the 40 under 40 Award from Pacific Business News.

the plight of the small-business owners. The exposure created a positive image of me as a credible and responsible person who understood broader issues. That reputation helped tremendously when I asked for loans or sought partners for our multimillion-dollar projects, especially for an under-funded small start-up company in a male-dominated industry such as real estate development.

Through the Chamber of Commerce I found like-minded people who cared about their business and cared about the well being of their employees and the community. As a result, we not only worked on healthcare issues, but we also found out that reducing the overall healthcare cost meant taking care of Hawai'i's uninsured. It became more than just trying to save a buck in business. As I met with non-profit organizations on healthcare issues, I discovered that workers compensation was another issue—healthcare-related, work-related—but it dealt with the masses. I reached out to employer groups, labor unions and politicians—people I would never normally talk with.

I met with union leaders to discover what it would require to fix what we felt were errors in the worker's compensation system. We tried to find solutions to a multitude of issues, including helping workers who were not receiving the kind of treatment they needed on a timely basis. We weren't as successful as we had hoped, but we were able to build a bridge of trust between groups that had rarely put confidence in each other before.

Now I find myself working on political issues that are beyond our businesses for the greater good of Hawai'i. It comes as a result of networking and working toward common causes. In one particular instance, a relationship with a union leader is helping me with my real estate development business. He finds allies who will help us to assist union workers in finding jobs, while making my job be cost-effective. Plus, with the help of non-profits, I have community alliances to help with my development projects. We are currently subsidizing an affordable rental housing project for at-risk, low-income people by building market homes supported by a non-profit group. These unintended results of networking helped my bottom line.

These win-win situations all came out of the basic desire to reduce my company's expenses and standing behind a cause that transcended to a greater purpose.

If you work with others for the greater good, it inevitably leads to a lifetime of relationships.

*"We're in a service business
and two things
are paramount:
number-one is results.
And number-two,
with results being a given,
is relationships."*

Nick Ng Pack
President and Chief Executive Officer
MILICI VALENTI NG PACK

Hollywood

Chris Lee, President, Chris Lee Productions

When I came [to Hollywood] from Hawai'i, I used every route I could to get myself in the door. That meant contacting people who had some vague relationship to somebody in the movie industry. And if I was lucky enough that they said, "Yes, come in and we'll do an interview," that's how I got a job.

But beyond that, I was very fortunate in connecting with a woman named Bonnie Lee, who graduated from Punahou. She is the sister of Edgy Lee, the famous filmmaker from Hawai'i. Bonnie was one of the top executives in Hollywood. She worked at Warner Brothers, where she was very much responsible for launching Tim Burton's career, and she very kindly agreed to meet with me.

Chris Lee is the president of Chris Lee Productions and former president of production for TriStar Pictures and Columbia Pictures. He worked on hits, such as *Jerry Maguire*, *My Best Friend's Wedding* and *The Patriot*. An Asian-American, Chris was the first minority to be president of production of a Hollywood studio. He founded the University of Hawai'i Academy for Creative Media and took four student interns to work on the blockbuster movie *Superman Returns*. Chris was consistently named one of the country's most influential Asian-Americans by *A Magazine*, served on the board of the National Asian Pacific American Legal Consortium in Washington D.C. and was a member of the Committee of 100.

Bonnie gave me a list of 11 individuals and she said, "Use my name, go and meet these people." I remember that 10 out of those 11 met with me. For whatever reason, the one person that couldn't meet with me, I remember clearly. Regardless of one bad rejection, though, it's truly the 10 that I got to spend time with that really started me networking in Hollywood.

I think I had some innate ability in terms of picking up material and analyzing; being able to be conversant in what hopefully would make a good movie or not make a good movie. But beyond that, it was absolutely essential that, through Bonnie Lee, I met agents, managers and other executives. They became a core group for me that was very supportive; and to this day, they are some of my best friends in Hollywood. They are the ones that I met in those very first few weeks at TriStar Pictures.

So I truly believe that one person can make a difference in a person's life ... through rejection one will gain motivation to keep going. On the flip-side, being introduced to others building relationships can last a lifetime.

*"As a leader,
you want to first off
develop a connection
with the people
that you're leading …
You have to let them know
that you care about them
and that you're interested
not only in their professional life
but also their personal life."*

Steven Hummer
Commanding General
MARINE CORPS BASE HAWAI'I (2005-2007)

Relationships vs. Transactions

Stephen B. Metter, President and Chief Executive Officer,
MW Group and Hawai'i Self Storage

If I were to distill it down, relationships are more important than transactions. Transactional activity builds taxable events, but relationships build sustainable wealth. Focus not only on deal points but consider all personalities and their needs and how to deliver the message. Incorporate this simple strategy into the decision-making process. Become relationship-centric.

Some of the largest MW Group acquisitions have all been relationship driven. I'll tell you three stories that greatly impacted our company's growth and validated my belief in the value of relationships over transactions.

The first is Pioneer Plaza. There were several buyers waiting for Pioneer Plaza to become available. The seller was represented by an experienced broker whom we had worked with in the past.

At the time, it was the biggest stand-alone asset we had attempted to acquire. There were other cash buyers who arguably were in a stronger financial position to close the transaction. With that said the broker had confidence in our ability to perform based on a personal relationship that had been established during previous smaller deals.

By August 2001 we had the property under contract. Then 9/11 hit, the terrorists flew a plane into the World Trade Center and the whole country stopped.

The broker called me and said, "Are we still going to close?"

I replied, "You know that my intention is to close; we need a couple of days

Stephen B. Metter is the CEO and principal of MW Group, Ltd. and MW Commercial Realty, Inc. MW Group, Ltd. is a diversified Hawai'i-based real estate development company with over $400 million in assets. Current holdings include office buildings, retail centers, Hawai'i Self Storage facilities, assisted-living centers and industrial complexes. Mr. Metter earned his Bachelor's Degree in Social Science from the University of California at Berkeley. Mr. Metter serves on the following boards: McDonald's Restaurants of Hawai'i, Pacific Rim Bank, Sennett Capital, Child and Family Services, Friends of Hawai'i State Art Museum, Hawaiian Humane Society, Fort Street Business Improvement District and Downtown Arts and Cultural District, The Plaza Club and is an active member of YPO.

Mr. Metter and his partner Michael B. Wood have built MW Group, Ltd. on a handshake; they have been partners since 1991.

to gather our thoughts, consult with the team and determine the willingness of the lender to advance the transaction." One week later the lender did modify their loan commitment requiring the seller to work with us to close the transaction. The deal closed on September 27, 2001, and we were informed that Pioneer Plaza was the first CBD office building to close post 9/11.

In the end, we relied on the strength of clear communication and the power of relationships to close the deal.

The second story is rooted in a very successful performance-driven relationship we have with the General Electric (GE) Capital real estate team. GE had its choice of buyers/developers who were pursuing a large shopping center portfolio they were selling. GE chose to do the deal with us because we were successful in a variety of past complicated GE asset repositionings. They placed a greater value on integrity, openness and performance than they did on cash at closing. We were able to structure a joint venture serving the long-term interests of both parties.

The GE relationship, like most good relationships, is based on honoring a series of small incremental challenges enabling both parties to prove themselves. So when a large opportunity becomes available you become the "go to" guys.

Lastly, the Plaza at Punchbowl assisted-living project was the direct benefit of a great relationship we have with Finance Factors. They knew we were looking for an infield location to build our first assisted-living facility. The real estate guys called offering us a potential home-run site provided we could close fast and ensure we would pay off the existing debt. We shook hands and the deal closed in less than 30 days. The Plaza at Punchbowl was extremely important to me, because I had made a promise to my father prior to his passing that we would build a high-quality rental assisted-living residence in Hawai'i. Finance Factors helped me keep that promise.

In summary, we have learned that transactions are only a nexus of change; building and maintaining relationships creates long-term value and sustainable wealth.

*"If you're not
a team player,
you're not going to
play on my team."*

David Carey
Chief Executive Officer
OUTRIGGER ENTERPRISES

Every Morning, Every Night

Jon de Mello, Founder and Chief Executive Officer, The Mountain Apple Company

Israel "Bruddah Iz" Kamakawiwʻoole [one of the major influences in Hawaiian music over the last 15 years], spent quite a bit of time at The Queen's Medical Center. Everyone was always anxiety ridden when he would land in a bed at Queen's [for weight-related illnesses due to his weight exceeding 800 lbs], but Israel considered it the Four Seasons Hotel. Everything was at his fingertips, if he rang for the nurse. Plus, he always had an audience at Queen's, even if his listeners were in their hospital gowns. He made the other patients feel better.

Queen's has special equipment for plus-size patients, and Israel always had this jungle-gym contraption around his bed so he could shift his weight around by grabbing a triangle attached to a galvanized pipe.

Jon de Mello is the founder and CEO of The Mountain Apple Company, the foremost leader in music recording, distribution, publishing, licensing and talent management in Hawaiʻi. In 2002, Jon became the first producer from a Hawaiʻi record label to have achieved an RIAA-certified gold record. In 2005, one of the records he produced was certified platinum. In the same year, he was instrumental in adding the Hawaiian Music category to the Grammy Awards, where Jon and his company represented three out of the five nominees. He has produced more than 150 recording projects that range from traditional Hawaiian to contemporary Island music. Jon stands as Hawaiʻi's biggest promoter of its music and culture to the global community.

In one of our meetings, I was at the foot of his bed, but I couldn't see his face clearly. I needed a way to communicate my point and understand his. We were talking, but there was little communication. Finally, I said "Israel, move over," and I climbed into bed right next to him. Our heads were on the pillow, but my feet barely reached his hips. It was quite a sight. At least we could turn and look at each other when making an important point.

This meeting lasted a few hours and when the nurses would walk in to do their job, they were totally flabbergasted and would react in very funny ways. This was one of the first of many very special moments I had with Israel.

He got into a habit of calling me first thing in the morning. He'd tell me a joke or a funny story, or we'd just talk. He was also the last one to call me at night. He was the only artist that I've ever worked with who'd call to thank me for how I had changed his life. On one thank-you call at 2 a.m., he sobbed uncontrollably and within seconds we were both in tears, arguing about who changed whose life more.

He called me his cheerleader. He nicknamed me "Yoda" after the *Star Wars* character. He was too humble to accept my constant chant of "they want your music, not me, Israel." I miss his calls, all of them.

We connected on many levels, and I believe his music demonstrates how well we worked together in the creative process. We trusted each other without ever having to say it out loud or prove it in a tangible way. It just worked.

This is what makes what I do for a living truly worthwhile. It's the opportunity to build priceless relationships with special people—that gives everything else meaning.

*"The key is partner first,
and partnership
(the business venture) second.
Good partners usually lead
to good partnerships,
so we spend a great deal of time
getting to know a partner
before entering a partnership."*

Allen Doane
Chairman and Chief Executive Officer
ALEXANDER & BALDWIN

Delivering More than Expected

Mitchell D'Olier, President and Chief Executive Officer, Kāne'ohe Ranch Company

Relationships are really important—they are the unstated assets on a balance sheet. And by over-delivering, relationships can span generations and the globe. For example, when I worked at Victoria Ward, we developed a relationship with Nordstrom Rack, the Seattle-based retail soft goods merchant. At the time, there was no Nordstrom Rack in Hawai'i, and Victoria Ward would be the first to welcome the retail concept to Hawai'i.

Through careful deliberation, both parties got to know each other and established a level of trust, which resulted in the signing of a lease contract. The key was our team's credibility and the integrity that we showed our retailers by treating them not as tenants, but as customers.

To fulfill our end of the deal, Victoria Ward prepared long and hard for the opening day of Nordstrom Rack. My team recalled how jammed up we got when Pier 1 Imports opened. We worried that Nordstrom Rack would create an even bigger stir. Since this was an important relationship for Victoria Ward, we decided that we should deliver more than what we promised on the contract, mainly to provide a smooth flow on opening day. We offered valet parking, extra security, traffic enforcers; we provided extra parking at the Neal Blaisdell Center and then ran shuttles to Victoria Ward. The team did a nice job of handling the traffic in and out the first couple of days, and that was something that was above and beyond what was required by Nordstrom's lease. Just as they try to surprise and delight customers, we tried to do the same.

Mitchell "Mitch" D'Olier is president and CEO of Kāne'ohe Ranch Company, Ltd. and a related non-profit foundation, The Harold K.L. Castle Foundation, the largest private foundation based in Hawai'i. Mitch has been in the forefront in shaping the landscape of Hawai'i. As president and CEO of Victoria Ward from 1993 to 2002, Mitch and the teams he worked with were instrumental in transforming Kaka'ako to a shopping and entertainment destination and the revitalization and renewal of the once-sleepy town of Kailua. He is actively involved in several community organizations, including Hawai'i Business Roundtable, Rotary Club of Honolulu, Boys & Girls Club of Hawai'i, Hawaiian Islands Ministries and The Oceanic Institute.

Since our team was smart enough to recognize potential problems and come up with solutions, we built a very strong, long-term relationship with Nordstrom. We not only kept our word, but we stayed within our construction timeline and we did not nickel-and-dime them once we accomplished our part of the deal. We built a real and positive connection with the Nordstrom Rack folks. That turned into a more important transaction, because Nordstorm Rack's then-president, Blake Nordstrom, became the president of Nordstrom, Inc., the parent company of the department store. This in turn led to a letter of intent to bring Nordstrom Shoe Store to Hawai'i through Ward and later to a department store letter of intent.

We've gained a lot of insight from our experience with Nordstrom Rack. All those who have worked with me took advantage of the opportunities that grew out of it. We have discovered that it's not only important to build relationships but that we also need to sustain them so that they carry on to other projects.

Now that I'm at Kāne'ohe Ranch Management Ltd. [which manages the Kailua real estate portfolio owned by the family trusts of Harold K.L. Castle and Alice H. Castle], I continue relationships with companies such as Pier 1 Imports and Nohea Gallery that have expanded from Kaka'ako to Kailua.

The experience at Ward is something I reflect on to this day at Kāne'ohe Ranch. The formula is simple: concentrate on building relationships, do your part at your end of the table and deliver more than what is expected of you.

*"It's truly imperative
to remember your relationships;
of paramount importance
are those relationships forged
in Hawai'i. Of course
one could also say that
friendships established
throughout the world
are very significant as well."*

Naomi Hazelton
Chief Executive Officer and Publisher
Pacific Edge Magazine

Relationship Currency

Bill Chee, Founder, Prudential Locations, LLC, and RESCO, Inc.

Relationships are an exchange. You have to offer something before you can get something back. Since you can't be good at everything, you have to build your own currency so that you have something to trade or exchange.

When you form a relationship with someone and they know that you respect their talent, they're more likely to like you because you genuinely admire and appreciate their skills, which are different from yours.

My concern is that people are never taught that. Everything in school is knowledge based; it's not relationship based. When you get out of school, everything is more relationship based than knowledge based. Life switches around on you as soon as you leave the academic world.

Everybody builds his or her own relationships. And you have to learn to enjoy someone who's different from you. You can't be too homogenous in terms of your friends. I knew a guy in real estate who was a good agent. One year he made 12 sales. Interestingly enough, out of those 12 sales, most of his customers were 32-year-old Japanese, who attended the University of Hawai'i. That's a narrow spectrum. You can imagine his life. However, when he held open houses, not everybody who came was 32 years old, attended the University of Hawai'i, and was Japanese; but that's how he saw the world.

On the other hand, one of my baselines is that I work with people who like results. All of my good friends and I hate process. We don't like to talk about the routine. We like to talk about

Bill Chee is the founder of Prudential Locations, LLC and RESCO Inc. and has stood as CEO of the companies since 1969. In 1976, at the age of 30, Bill served simultaneously as the president of the Hawai'i Association of Realtors and the Honolulu Board of Realtors. In 1993, he served as the president of the National Association of Realtors and has been the only ethnic minority to fill the position. The Hawai'i Association of Realtors and Honolulu Board of Realtors honored Bill as Realtor of the Year in 1976 and 1991. He is the director for a number of organizations, including Hawai'i National Bank, Institute of Human Services and National Association of Realtors. He also serves on the Real Estate Commission for the state of Hawai'i.

how to do things, strategies and key points versus the hundreds of points. Even though we may not have the same personalities, skills and talents, we do have to share a destination. We're always on this trip. Everybody thinks the same way. We believe in loyalty. We believe in affiliations. We believe in sharing.

Sometimes friends influence you. They show you things that you didn't see before or they provide new insights. The neat thing about it is that you can borrow somebody else's experience, knowledge, education and relationships. It's wonderful when you have someone to serve as your guide.

One example of this was with a friend of 25 years. Little did I know that a candid conversation would turn into a close friendship. He passed away at 86 years old, but he was a key friend for two decades. He guided and encouraged me to further my career. If it wasn't for that relationship, I don't think I would have become president of the National Association of Realtors. He chose to be my mentor because I think he saw my potential to become a leader, but only because I reflected what I saw in him as a role model. There was a mutual benefit in that respect.

The way we became friends was in no way a technical approach. When you're building a relationship, you and the other person simply engage in a dialogue. Before you know it, you're talking about all kinds of things. Friendships aren't built with the intention of "using" people, but they often benefit you in unexpected ways.

Relationships are spontaneous and uncontrollable; that's why you have to cherish every rapport that you've built along the way. You can't just say, "I'm dealing with all these smart people because I'm going to need them someday." You have to have something to give in return, whatever that may be, so that the relationship will flourish.

I've been fortunate that other people's talents intrigue me, so I don't get jealous or judge it. I view it as, "Hey, that's really cool ... they can do something that I can't do."

I admire guys like my friend, Stanley Hong. He gets along with everybody. I've watched him work a room and talk to everyone.

I think to myself, "Wow, what a talent!"

Consider relationships as currency that doesn't depreciate in value. When you know how to establish rapport, build a connection based on trust and respect. Your relationships with people will even appreciate over time.

*"Make sure that you
tend to your 'ohana (family),
because it's your 'ohana
that tends to you
when you bump into
the really tough problems
in life."*

David Cole
Chairman, President and Chief Executive Officer
MAUI LAND & PINEAPPLE COMPANY

6

THE IMPORTANCE OF FAMILY

6

THE IMPORTANCE OF FAMILY

Evan Leong, Chief Executive Officer, Greater Good Inc.

I'm writing this on my flight back from the Philippines. I've been trying to sleep but am one of those people who just can't seem to do it. Although this is one of the the last chapters of the book's introductions I'm working on, that's not really why I put it off until the end. Instead, I think it's because I don't truly believe that I've been particularly strong in this area. However, there's nothing like an 11-hour flight to allow for self-reflection.

For years, I was totally focused on building my business career, using the excuse that I was doing it for my family. In truth, it was more for my own ego. Realizing this is an eye-opening revelation.

During the first part of the flight I watched the movie *Click*, starring Adam Sandler. When it was over, I had to watch it again. If you haven't seen the film, I recommend it. It's basically about a guy who is trying so hard to become a partner in his architectural firm that he puts his family off to please his boss and further his career. Then he is given a universal remote control that allows him to control his life. He can fast-forward through unpleasant situations, mute the volume on things he doesn't want to hear and go back and forth in time. He essentially goes through life on automatic pilot, watching his career skyrocket while his family relationships deteriorate. His wife divorces him and remarries. He misses the early years with his kids, who don't want to spend any time with him when they're older. He hurts his father emotionally and isn't there when he passes away. At the end, he wakes up and realizes it was all a dream. Lucky for him, he gets a second chance. Unfortunately, this is reality for many people, and most will not get a second chance.

I couldn't help watching this movie and seeing myself in it. Like Sandler's character, I "woke up," and I'm willing to make the necessary changes. It's a reminder that sometimes we need to take one step back for every two steps forward—to look closely at our lives and where we're headed, and decide if we're willing to accept that or try for something better instead. Our families deserve this.

It's easy to forget family time in our quest for business success and our place in the world. The realization is that no amount of material gain can replace a broken home. Being the richest person in the graveyard has no real value. Central Pacific Bank president Clint Arnoldus puts it this way: "I've never seen a hearse followed by an armored car."

My family has been a driving force behind any success that I've achieved, especially in business. My father helped Kari and me get bank loans for our first business. Kari's family helped us with trade shows, deliveries and whatever else we needed help with. Our family is the backbone of our success.

In our interviews on Greater Good Radio and TV we pose a series of questions to each guest, in order to collect and compare the answers. One of them is, "What is your greatest life accomplishment?" The consistency of the answers is overwhelming. More than 90 percent mentioned their family and especially their children. A few examples:

> "If you raise two children, three children, or even four children and they go off into this world and have the ability to make a contribution, I don't think that there's anything more rewarding than that."
> — Admiral Thomas Fargo, *Admiral (USN Ret.), CEO,* TREX ENTERPRISES

> "My greatest life accomplishment is my family; I'm proud of my family, my wife, and all of my children who I think are going to be model citizens and hopefully will also be good entrepreneurs and mentors to younger people."
> — Bert Kobayashi, *Chairman,* THE KOBAYASHI GROUP

> "I would have to say my sons are my biggest accomplishment because they bring me incredible joy and I'm very, very proud of them. Very, very great kids!"
> — Crystal Rose, *Partner,* BAYS, DEAVER, LUNG, ROSE & HOLMA

"I think raising my four children, and to see what they've become and to see them raising their children in a similar way, may be the single most gratifying thing in my life."
— Captain Jerry Coffee, *Captain (USN Ret.)*, CEO, COFFEE ENTERPRISES

"My kids—Bryson, 16, Jarrod, 12, and Lauren, 2. I still look at that and do I think it's my accomplishment? No. I think I've had the opportunity to learn from them because I think that kids are our greatest teachers. They teach me more than I think I'm teaching them."
— Mike McCartney, *Chairman*, DEMOCRATIC PARTY OF HAWAI'I

"Without question it's being able to have six kids and all those grandkids and seeing every one of them really active, productive citizens of our country. They are hardworking, they have good values and just to see that carry through is very, very rewarding."
— Clint Arnoldus, *President and CEO*, CENTRAL PACIFIC BANK

"Building my family. I have a wonderful wife who is a second grade teacher, who's been there for over 20 years, and I have a three-year-old daughter and an eight-month-old son and they're just the joy of my life and they make my work more relevant and personal—and they make me fall in love with all kids. I want to make sure Hawai'i's future is great for all kids. My family inspires me to do that work."
— Terrence George, *Executive Director*, HAROLD K.L. CASTLE FOUNDATION

"My biggest life accomplishment? I think I have the respect of my three children. That runs really deep for me, and with them, and despite the fact that we went through some tumultuous times. I think knowing that is real important."
— Rick Blangiardi, *President and General Manager*, KGMB9 TV

"Number one was when I got married to my lovely wife, and number two was when she gave birth to our son."
— General Steven Hummer, *Commander*, MARINE CORPS BASE HAWAI'I (2005-2007)

"It would start with family, so obviously my wife of 30-something years ... I have two wonderful daughters and the most wonderful things I can say about both those girls are that they have wonderful values. And what more can a parent ask for? It starts with family."
— John Dean, *Partner*, STARTUP CAPITAL VENTURES

Interestingly enough, the number one regret that our interviewees have is not spending enough time with their kids when they are young. We can always spend money and make it back but we can never get back time with our kids and family.

In November 2006, friends and family gathered at my aunt's house for dinner. My auntie's cancer had been in remission, and she just learned that the cancer had returned. The doctors told her that she would have one year to live and she wanted a second opinion, so she decided to go to Houston, Texas, where there is a special cancer clinic and research facility. This was especially hard on my uncle, whose mother had just passed away. Her funeral was moved back a few weeks to allow time for the Houston trip. Our entire family said their prayers that Auntie would beat the cancer again. I told her that I would see her when she got back. Unfortunately, the unexpected happened. Traveling from Hawai'i to Houston was extremely hard on my aunt. She got sick during the flight, which led to pneumonia. She fell into a coma and passed away a few days later.

I attended two funerals in the same month, at the same church, for the same family. My uncle lost his mother and wife within two weeks. I was an usher for both funerals, but the funeral for my aunt was the hardest I've ever attended. When the funeral is for someone fairly young, you naturally feel they were cheated out of a full life. All of this was a wake-up call for me, a reminder that we never know how long we have here on Earth.

After an especially tiring day of funeral activities we ended up at my uncle's house for dinner. He said something to me that night that really made me think. "It feels like I'm dreaming," he said, holding back tears with extreme sadness in his eyes. "I can't help but think that I'm going to wake up tomorrow morning, pinch myself and realize it's all a bad dream. But I know that's not going to happen. I know she's gone. I would give anything for just a little more time with her. Tell your wife every day that you appreciate her and love her."

We never know how much time we will be allowed to live our lives. There's nothing like the death of a family member or close friend to make us appreciate our families. That's the time when families tend to get really close. That's the time people forget about their differences and come together. What if every day was like that? What if we took care of our family as if our time together was coming to an end, as it inevitably must?

Even though family responsibilities can be difficult to balance, especially for those in business, they're also what's most important. We regret the things we don't attempt much more than we do when we try something and fail. We owe it to our family to give them the best effort possible. I hope that the stories in this chapter will remind you to cherish and appreciate the moments with your family daily, weekly, monthly—always.

*"In terms of
life accomplishments,
the smartest thing
I ever did was
marry my wife, Lynn."*

Jeffrey N. Watanabe
Non-Executive Chair
HAWAIIAN ELECTRIC INDUSTRIES
Founding Partner
WATANABE ING & KOMEIJI

Riding a Bike

Robin K. Campaniano, President and Chief Executive Officer,
AIG Hawai'i Insurance Company

I don't like to look back on my life and rethink how I would change something. I'd much prefer looking toward the future. However, one thing I have never done enough of is spend time with my family. We all say that family is important, but I don't think one could spend too much time with loved ones. I know I haven't spent enough time with my children. Now that they're older, I'm glad they turned out to be as grounded as they are despite my frequent absences. As the State Insurance Commissioner I was always attending meetings and conferences, giving speeches. It was heady stuff, presenting remarks at Lloyd's of London one week, testifying in Congress the next and flying off to Tokyo a few weeks later.

One Saturday, I was returning home from the East Coast and riding in the back seat of a taxi, scribbling notes for a speech I was to give the following Wednesday in Washington, D.C. As we pulled up in my driveway, my wife came out and said, "Don't come into the garage. I have a surprise for you."

I thought to myself. "Oh my, what's this all about?"

My two kids came out of the garage riding their two-wheel bikes.

I said, in astonishment, "How did they do that?"

She told me that she had taken the kids down to Isenberg Park and she was pushing them on their bikes with training wheels when a custodian came over and helped teach the kids how to ride without the training wheels.

Robin K. Campaniano is president and CEO of AIG Hawai'i Insurance Company and Hawai'i Insurance Consultants. He is also chairman and CEO of 50th State Risk Management and American Pacific Insurance Company. Robin was the insurance commissioner for the state of Hawai'i between 1987 to 1991. He is a director of First Hawaiian Bank and an advisor to Oceanic Cablevision. He has received the Ernst & Young Entrepreneur of the Year, University of Hawai'i Distinguished Alumni and Outstanding Public Schools Graduate awards. Robin is involved with numerous non-profit boards including Hawai'i Children's Discovery Center, HMSA Foundation and Public Schools of Hawai'i Foundation. He is a recipient of the March of Dimes Franklin D. Roosevelt Award for Distinguished Community Service.

At that point, I realized the consequences of too much emphasis on work.

Teaching kids how to ride a bike was a dad's job, not a park custodian's. I was proud of the kids' accomplishments, but it felt hollow as I didn't participate in the process.

I cancelled my upcoming trip, didn't give the speech I had been working on, and shortly thereafter, left my position. It taught me a lesson about balancing work, family and everything else in life.

Make sure you spend the time with loved ones while you can. You can never spend too much time with your wife and children. If your family life is balanced, everything else will follow. Since making a change and trying to be more balanced, I've noticed a difference in how I feel when I am at work and when I am with my family. I treasure each moment because I will never get it back.

*"As a businesswoman
and a woman entrepreneur
striving for success, I realized
that a woman has to really be honest
with herself about her role
in the family and decisions
about children, whether she's
going to have children
and if she does, can she accept
the fact that the majority
of the waking hours the child may
be taken care of by somebody else?"*

Christine Camp
Founder and Chief Executive Officer
AVALON DEVELOPMENT COMPANY

Knowledge and Discipline

Brian Keaulana, Co-Founder and Partner, C4 Waterman

I come from a long line of legendary Hawaiians, my father being Buffalo Keaulana. He taught us how to not only enjoy the ocean but to read and respect it—everything that a Hawaiian waterman is. His greatest gifts to us were his knowledge and discipline.

We lived a simple life growing up at Mākaha Beach. My father had a horse and from time to time we rode with him, picking up rubbish on the beach and putting it into a satchel bag.

My father was a park keeper back then. There were no official lifeguards back then, but he ended up making a lot of rescues, bringing people out of the water. Because he saved so many lives, the mayor appointed him the first lifeguard on the west side.

When my father wasn't in the ocean, he focused on our family. He raised my sister and me with tools to survive in and out of the water.

I remember my father throwing us into the ocean current. People thought he was mean. But he was really on our side, teaching us how to get out of the current.

The waves would be big and his friends would ask him, "Why do you do that to your kids?"

He would say, "One day I might not be here, and they might get caught and not know how to get out."

I remember one day when Mākaha's surf was really big and this guy was caught in a rip current and was yelling for help. I got off the lifeguard tower and started running. My father was also on the tower, but he didn't react the way that I did. I ran down the beach toward the guy and then heard my dad's whistle. All of us boys knew that when you hear that whistle (it seems like you could hear it from miles away), you stop

Brian Keaulana is co-founder and partner in C4 Waterman. He has been both in front of the camera and behind it as a professional stunt man and stunt coordinator for 20 years. Brian has been featured in numerous films, such as *Riding Giants* and *Billabong Odyssey*. He was the stunt coordinator for major Hollywood productions *Pipeline* and *Blue Crush*, among many others. Brian participates in almost every professional waterman competition and was awarded the 2007 World Tandem Surfing Championship. Brian grew up on the beach at Mākaha, one of the most famous surf spots in Hawai'i. His passion is deeply rooted in modern ocean safety and ancient Hawaiian culture.

dead in your tracks.

I looked back at my dad, and he waved and said, "Wait, hang on."

He walked toward me real slow. I stood there freaking out that this guy might drown.

"What is my dad stopping me for? I can go get him," I thought to myself.

My dad walked to the edge of the sand embankment and looked at the guy.

The guy was yelling for help and his wife ran up to us screaming, "Save my husband!"

My dad said, "No, not yet."

I'm thinking, "Wow, my dad is nuts."

As the wife flipped out, my father just waited. Finally, he looked at the guy and he yelled, "Stand up!"

The guy was treading water and shouted, "What?"

"Stand up!" my father yelled again.

Then the guy's wife shouted, "He said to stand up!"

Then the guy stood up and he walked out of the water.

After the experience, my dad told him, "OK, now you know how to get out of the current. Drift across the water, and when you get to the sand bar, just stand up."

My dad walked away like it was no big thing. In later years, I realized that my dad made a rescue without rescuing. He empowered this guy with knowledge to save himself.

After learning how to ride the current on our own, my sister and I played games and made trouble to the unsuspecting tourists. We would jump into the ocean and ride the current. Tourists would stop by and think, "Look at these kids. They're having fun."

They would end up joining us, but almost drown.

My dad would get mad because he knew we were enjoying our game at the expense of others. These are great memories, but when we put others in danger, we didn't get away without any form of disciplinary action.

I was fortunate and lucky that I learned discipline growing up.

But I think nowadays we forget about discipline.

Today, someone's child can easily say, "I'm going to sue you, Dad. I'm going to sue you, Mom."

Back then, it was just one crack (physical reminder) and that was all it took for you to say, "OK, I understand."

Society has changed, and sometimes the intentions are good. But then again, I feel that many of our values have been lost. I strive not to let that happen in my family. I try to instill my parents' values in my own kids. I try to spend a lot of time with them, allowing them to grow and experience a similar life that I did.

I'm lucky that my father is an active part of his grandchildren's lives and helps me raise them. He has 10 grandkids and he takes them all to the beach to swim. One day I was looking out the window and saw this long serpent-like shadow underwater.

I asked myself, "What is that?" It didn't look like anything I'd seen before in the water. Whatever it was, it was snaking its way in the shoreline. Suddenly it pops up and I realized that it was my father, with all 10 grandkids hanging onto his legs. He was playing with one of those Jacques Cousteau submersibles that I had bought him.

That is the thing that I appreciate—that my kids, my nephews and nieces all have the opportunity to experience many of the same values (and fun). The Wai'anae side of the island is a magical place for us. Everyone knows everyone there. It's a small, tightly knit community. Everyone works together, lives together, fishes together and plays together. We all share the value of 'ohana, or family, and we watch out for each other.

"I am not just in business because of my family, but also for my family."

Josh Feldman
President and Chief Executive Officer
TORI RICHARD, LTD.

Perpetuating the Next Generation

T. Michael May, President and Chief Executive Officer, Hawaiian Electric Company, Inc.

My dad was a man of few words, but his simple lessons and sayings have been guideposts throughout my life. For example, "I don't care if you run a company, become an artist or be a technician," my dad said. My dad never had any specific professional expectations of me.

He never said, "We will love you more if you're successful in life."

"All I ask is that you apply yourself to the best of your ability and do it with good character," he also said. "That's all we would ever ask of you."

Those little snippets, or sound bytes, resonate in me. I try to pass the same ideals to my children.

As you give your children the freedom to make their own decisions, you have to make sure that you provide them lessons, morals and values early on so that they make informed and just choices as adults.

A lot of times, those lessons are taught not by what you say but what you do.

My dad was a Quaker by upbringing. Quakers are very strict. And I am a product of that stringent environment. I was a kid that needed guidance. Both of my parents provided it.

My parents made sure that along with the rigid rules, they provided life lessons so that I could develop into a man with good character.

For example, when I turned 16 years old, my priority was get a car and then get a girlfriend. As a teenager, the car would provide me territory and freedom to roam it.

So I made a deal with my dad that he'd get me a car as long as I kept up my grades.

Mike May is the president and CEO of Hawaiian Electric Company, the largest utility provider in the state of Hawai'i. Mike is also chairman to the advisory boards of directors of Maui Electric Company, Ltd. and Hawai'i Electric Light Company, Inc. Prior to joining HECO, he founded a management-consulting firm called Management Assets Group. From 1981 to 1989, Mike served as president and vice president for Caterpillar's independent power production and industrial gas turbine manufacturing subsidiaries respectively. Mike holds a bachelor's degree in Industrial Management, with further training in industrial engineering from the University of Mississippi. He also holds a master's degree in finance from The College of William and Mary.

My first report card came out just after getting the car and I had failed to keep my end of the deal. I left the house the next morning to go to school in my car and it was gone. There was no discussion. He sold it out from under me.

Dad gave me another chance with another car. But the same thing happened; I let my grades slip. He sold that car out from under me, too. I learned accountability the hard way, one car at a time. He told me, "You don't get it. We're going to keep doing this routine until you understand that you need to keep your end of the bargain."

Words of wisdom passed on from generation to generation. Another lesson from my dad that has served me well is, "If you don't have a plan, you're going to be part of somebody else's."

What he taught me at an early age was clear: set standards, stick to them and work from there. I have come to realize that the more complex the situation, the tougher it can be to do the right thing. Whenever I question a decision or choice, I think about what my dad would do. He taught me about integrity, not through what he said but by his actions. At an early age I learned by his living example.

I saw my dad go out of his way to care for the family of one of his retired employees, who had a serious, long-term health problem. He delivered Thanksgiving and Christmas meals to make sure that the family could celebrate the holidays.

I often observed him in his business dealings, too. I learned that he put honesty and integrity above achieving wealth. If there were ever choices between a huge financial success and doing the right thing, I would say, without exception, he would do the right thing.

As I started my own family, it was important to me to teach my children lessons, as my father did for me. I felt like he did a good job and I've asked him, "How could I ever repay you for the lessons that you've taught me and for the support you have given me in life?"

"You can't," he said. "The only thing you can do is to give your kids the same kind of help, support and guidance that I gave you."

I've come to realize that parenting is a very challenging and interesting process. You don't get a report card on parenting until it's too late. You invest in your kids with experiences and education. You think you're doing the right thing in the first grade, the right thing in intermediate school, the right thing in high school, then you wake up one day and they're out on their own. They're making independent choices and decisions. The moments of affirmation that you were a responsible, good parent are evident. For example, when you watch your kid marching on college graduation day, you see that the discipline paid off. Seeing my daughter survive the college experience and graduate was very satisfying.

I also exposed the kids to sports and a host of other things. I wanted to let them know that life is a menu. You get to pick from a variety of things, which lead to a collective success.

Planting values by example and by word, and shaping healthy environments are critical factors when children are growing up. For instance, our kids grew up in the church, because we wanted them to have a framework from which to make decisions. It's not just right or wrong; it's a value proposition. At times, when I'm not available, I have the assurance that my kids are in the right setting, in the right environment, getting the right kind of influences.

This is the kind of parenting that I do, which was modeled after my father. I've come to realize that it's the circle of life; we continue to perpetuate the next generation.

*"My family is my primary
motivating force ...
Ultimately, I measure my success
by the amount of time
I am able to dedicate
to my family."*

John Otterson
Managing Director
SVB CAPITAL

My Mom

Lincoln Jacobe, President and Chief Executive Officer, Hawai'i Pacific Entertainment

My parents were teenagers when I was born, so they were still figuring out who they were while they raised me. The three of us grew up together and eventually it became just the two of us—me and Mom. My mom was and is my best friend. Because we were always close, I listened to her throughout my life and turned to her as a mentor.

It wasn't always easy for my mom to raise me, especially during my teenage years. These were the times when I wanted to experience drugs and alcohol—they were easily accessible in my neighborhood. Involvement in that world changed me as a person and gave me a reality check early in life.

I remember the day clearly. I was with a friend who was a drug dealer in Kalihi and Chinatown. We were buying drugs in the Chinatown Cultural Plaza parking lot and all of a sudden one of my friends pulled out a gun.

I asked, "What is the gun for?"

"This might be a bad deal," he said.

That's when I freaked out. I was really shocked that there was a gun and my life was in jeopardy. After that day, I swore that I would not hang around with those friends again.

This was a really challenging time because my choices and activities caused friction at home. My mother always tried to rope me back to her and keep me close.

As I continued to figure out who I was and who I wanted to become, my mother did her best to provide for me mentally, physically and emotionally. She was aware of the choices and mistakes I made along the way and she

Lincoln Jacobe is the founder and CEO of Hawai'i Pacific Entertainment, a Honolulu-based company since 1996 that specializes in media, communications & entertainment. Focus areas of concentration include sports & entertainment management and marketing, television, film & video production and casting. The company also focuses on special event management, publicity, promotions and productions. Jacobe is also the founder and CEO of the Technology News Network, Hawai'i's largest technology news, information & events organization, offering the latest buzz in tech through television, radio, print, broadcast, events and on-line distribution channels. Jacobe also founded a non-profit organization, The Pacific Technology Foundation, which offers technology scholarships and computers for schools, teachers and students.

continually reminded me of the right path and how my choices would lead to consequences. She wanted to make sure that I wouldn't get stuck in the same situation, being poor, my whole life. She pushed me to get the most out of the public school system and excel in education.

Because of my mom's push to study hard in school, I carried that dedication into my work ethic.

At age 15, I got my first job at McDonald's. Eventually I took a second job. After graduating from Farrington High School I took on a third job. My mother always taught me the importance of living frugally, working hard and saving money, which I did. I saved all of my earnings and put a down payment on my first condo when I was 19 years old. This was a huge milestone in my life. I saw that working hard and saving money gave me freedom.

From that point on, I knew that I was not going to be pigeonholed in the area that I grew up in, Kalihi. I wanted to become a successful person and make enough money so that I could buy things that I never had as a kid. For example, new clothes instead of used clothes from the thrift shops. Not only did I want a better life for myself, I wanted it for my mother, too. As a young girl, my mom grew up under similar circumstances, but she wasn't able to break the cycle, especially as a young wife and mother.

I broke the cycle, but I did not do it on my own. I did it with my mother's love. I didn't have a lot of material things when I was growing up, but I was rich in the love I received from my mom. She really loved me because I was her only child. She taught me how to be strong. She always supported me and encouraged me whenever I needed her. She taught me lessons along the way about how to deal with people: do unto others as they do unto you. She said that she would always be there for me, and she was.

When I started my business, it was scary, but my mom was very supportive. Now, I share my success celebrations with her so that she can also experience my achievements. It's because of her that I am who I have become today. Her love and support have kept me strong and on track, moving forward and keeping everything in a positive direction. We don't live in the past; we just look at what's ahead.

*"We all work for a reason.
We work for our family.
If you don't have
that quality time with
your family and your children,
it makes the hard work
less meaningful."*

John Bower
Co-Founder and Managing Partner
SENNET CAPITAL

A GRANDMOTHER'S LOVE

Allen Doane, Chairman and Chief Executive Officer, Alexander & Baldwin

My grandmother has been the central influence in my life. If I have accomplished anything good, it is because of her. Of course, my flaws are of my own creation. Let me start at the beginning.

My grandmother had seven children, with my mother being the youngest. She raised these seven children during the Great Depression of the 1930s. It was especially difficult for her as she raised all seven children on her own because her husband, my grandfather, abandoned her. Times were tough for my mother and her six siblings, growing up in Philadelphia. When I came along in the late 1940s, my grandmother was in her early 60s, and she took much of the responsibility of raising me. In a neighborhood that could be generously described as "working class" (the euphemism for the category under middle class), three of my aunts and uncles lived within a city block of my grandmother. Even then, getting by was a day-in and day-out challenge for my grandmother. Her home was a rooming house where men lived on a weekly or monthly basis—an apartment of sorts. As a small child I would help her clean the rooms, and I can vividly recall using my little shovel several times a day to help her put coal in a boiler for heat in the winter. These were happy times!

I barely graduated from a public high school in Philadelphia. As I worked 30 to 40 hours a week during high school, there was no time for sports or academics. With this background, there wasn't much hope of going to college. Then a series of events occurred that fundamentally changed my life.

Upon graduating from high school, I got a job as a busboy in the cafeteria of

Allen Doane takes charge of one of Hawai'i's largest and most successful companies, Alexander & Baldwin, Inc. As chief executive officer, chairman of the board, president and director of the 125-year-old diversified corporation, Allen has led his company to incredible heights, reaching revenues of more than $1.6 billion in 2006, and a market capitalization in excess of $2 billion. Allen engages actively in the community as member of the board of several organizations. His company has given more than $4 million to charities in Hawai'i and the Pacific in the last two years, and has impacted communities in dire need of help.

a big downtown Philadelphia office building. As strange as it sounds, it opened my eyes up to a world of possibilities that I had never considered. It was already well into summer before I decided to think about college. Through various means, I identified several schools that had late acceptance periods. Brigham Young University (BYU) accepted me on a probationary status. While not a member of the Mormon faith, nor having more than a vague idea where Utah was located, I decided to give college a try.

The most meaningful part of this story involves my grandmother, who gave me a large part of her meager savings so I could attend college. At that time, she was 77 and still working to maintain a rooming house in her home. As the years have gone by, my appreciation for her tremendous sacrifice for me has deepened. From my earliest memories of childhood through a college education, she was always there for me. Having endured the Great Depression while raising seven children by herself, she had more than enough love to raise a grandson, too.

*"The number-one memory
I have of my mother is
the strong love and support
she has always provided me
from as early as I can remember
growing up as a child."*

Lincoln H. Jacobe
Founder & Chief Executive Officer
HAWAI'I PACIFIC ENTERTAINMENT

Success Is Family Stability

Salevaa "Konishiki" Atisanoe, Sumo Champion and Entrepreneur

Sometimes people ask me the question "What is success to you?" To me, true success is when I know everyone in my family is stable, financially and emotionally. My first mission is to get everyone in my family to lead a comfortable lifestyle and, secondly, to be home in Hawai'i, where there's so much that can be done to help other people.

I feel much better when I can do something for somebody. I like to give to my family, because we grew up as less-privileged members of the community, but my parents never showed that. They taught us to do as much as we could with what we had and to help other people.

Growing up, my parents taught and lead by example how to be positive. My dad has helped a lot of Samoan families start their lives here in Hawai'i, from getting their citizenship to getting jobs. This was how I got this sense of charity.

My family has always been my greatest influence and driving force. The inspiration they have given me to get up as I falter is much greater than the support I give to them today. I realized how fortunate I am to have my family during my toughest days in Japan. During the debate about whether I, being a foreigner, should be made a grand champion or not, somebody accused me of saying that Japan was a racist country, when in fact it was only the sumo officials that I derided. The news spread like wildfire all over the world. They had it in the front page in the *New York Times* that the Japanese prime minister came out on TV on the news to say, "No that is not true, Japan is not a racist country."

Going back to Japan from Hawai'i at that time, I got a phone call from a friend.

Konishiki made a name for himself in the Japanese sport of sumo wrestling by winning his first consecutive 23 matches and becoming the first foreign-born to reach the rank of Ozeki, or champion. During his career, which started in 1982, he won the top division championship on three occasions and paved the way for other foreign-born wrestlers to become grand champion, or Yokozuna. Born Salevaa Fauali Atisanoe, Konishiki's talents are not restricted to athleticism. He is also an established recording artist, with more than half a dozen albums, and he owns a restaurant called Unbalanced in Tokyo, Japan. Konishiki is also the founder of Konishiki Kids Foundation and is involved in various community-based, youth-oriented initiatives.

"Don't come to the stable," he said.

I asked, "Why?"

"There are about 200 members of the media waiting outside to interview you."

"About what?" I asked.

I didn't understand what was going on and what was to come out of it.

The events that were taking place were blown out of proportion; it hurt me so bad that I could not focus. It was so bad that I was thinking about committing suicide. I could not face the problem because I would be further blamed. Plus, the Sumo Association and even my stable, which I thought were my big supporters, did not back me up. Everybody was just covering their own butts. No one wanted to be part of what was truly happening—even to the point where they made me go on TV and apologize for something that I did not do.

But I was lucky that I had my family to turn to in this time of great despair. I called my mom every day, telling her about my feelings, and she told me, "Come home, just come home already," which I couldn't do because I thought that would be giving up and letting them win the battle.

This was one of the rare moments that I called home to share the troubles I was going through in Japan. Before this, I had never shared my hardships with my family. Even when I got injured, they would find out only through the newspaper that I was in the hospital. I never let them know that side of my career. Plus, it would have been very hard to explain to anybody the lifestyle we lived in Japan, especially to them. Being Samoan-cultured made it even harder for them to understand. I had a hard time comprehending my own situation. The support that my family gave me through those tumultuous times was enough for me to see the bright light out of all the darkness.

After things settled, I tried hard to get back my passion for the sport. I loved it before, but I put so much pressure on myself to win all the time. I've learned through my family not to worry about the winning—just go do it, enjoy it and love it and it would last forever.

By learning to love sumo, I have come to consider myself the messenger for which my parents prayed. I was the baby of the family, yet I was put in the position to make our lives better. I saw my parents busting their butts when they were young. No one grumbled over the canned goods that came that day, because that's the canned goods the whole family was going to eat. We ate canned sardines and mackerel almost every day, yet nobody grumbled because my parents were good leaders in the household. Outside, at church, they were very strong leaders and I always looked to them for the best advice. Sometimes people do not notice that some of the best advice they can find is right there next to them.

My family keeps me going, and the sense of mutual giving and respect makes our bond even stronger.

My foundation is my family, and that is what drives me to do good, not only for them but also for other people. I try to help children in my own way by enforcing a family-oriented philosophy. The kids that come out of a good upbringing are the ones who are more head-cool and try to take care of their families.

It is very important for kids to understand at a young age not to let their impoverished state hold them back from what they want to be. I have been there; I am a living proof and I know there is a positive way out.

When I left 25 years ago, our family did not have shower rooms, and we did not have a kitchen in the house, but we did not care about that. It did not stop us from trying to be good in whatever we put ourselves in. I try to share my story and explain to the children today what I went through with the hope of influencing them to do good. I think there are more than enough people who can be successful in this community if they are guided right and believe that they can make it. That's why our families are so important.

*"The real turning point
came when my
prayers finally changed
from, "Why me, God?" to
"Show me, God."*

Captain Jerry Coffee (USN Ret.)
Chief Executive Officer
COFFEE ENTERPRISES

7

UNDENIABLE
FAITH

7

UNDENIABLE FAITH

Evan Leong, Chief Executive Officer, Greater Good Inc.

More than a few people raised their eyebrows when I mentioned that there would be a chapter in this book about faith. The truth of the matter is that I don't think my businesses—or my life—would be anywhere close to where they are now without faith. Now, that doesn't necessarily mean religion. It means faith in something that is greater than we are. This thought was also voiced by many of the leaders we have interviewed.

I once heard a seminar speaker discuss faith. He said that he used to be an atheist until he met one very successful person. When he told this person he didn't believe in a higher power of some sort, the response was, "So you think that you are the Supreme Being then? If you don't believe in something greater than yourself, you believe that you are the ultimate."

That has stuck with me until this day. I know that I'm only a very small part of a much larger plan. I just pray that I can live up to the things I need to do in order to fulfill my purpose. The only way I see that happening is with faith. Faith has changed my life. I attribute my business success to my wife, Kari, and I attribute meeting my wife to faith.

Kari is fairly soft-spoken, a real sweetheart. In most social settings I'm the one who's more talkative, outgoing and extroverted. My aunties always tell me, "You're so lucky to have a girl like Kari; you're just lucky." They often use the word "luck." I guess you could say it was luck; however, I would give much more credit to the faith that created the luck.

In the winter of 1995 I was working with a company that had an office in Orem, Utah. This was a time when I was supposed to be doing really well with the company, but in reality, things were mediocre at best. I wondered if I should be doing something else, but I'd worked so hard that I didn't want to quit. That year I decided that I didn't want to come home for Christmas.

At the time I was living in a rented room that I shared with a friend. The room was maybe 10 feet by 10 feet. My roommate was a big Samoan guy who weighed more than 300 pounds and stood 6'2". We had two beds, side by side, almost touching each other. There was a small area to store our clothes and the few things we owned, and we shared a bathroom with another roommate in our two-bedroom apartment.

Spending time away from family during the holidays in virtual seclusion is pretty depressing. It was then that I became more in touch with myself and realized that I had drifted from my faith because I was so engulfed in my work. I decided that I had to re-prioritize my goals in life and my relationships. I wanted a serious relationship with a woman who had all the qualities I wanted, a woman I could fall in love with. I had a lot of time to think and I wrote a long list of everything I wanted in a woman—emotionally, physically, socially, mentally and spiritually. It must have been 10 pages long.

Then I said a prayer over the list—a really strong and sincere prayer. I prayed and prayed on it. I put a deadline on my goals: "I will meet this person by June 1, 1996, and we will start a relationship which will lead to marriage."

In early 1996 I left Utah to come back home to Hawai'i, and it just so happened that my friend Kekoa had his birthday party at a house he was selling. It was the end of May and that's where I initially met Kari. We talked, started dating and began working together. In 1998 we were married. It's been a really incredible partnership. I don't think it was so much luck as a testament of faith. I believe that she is the answer that God gave to my prayers. We now have two young boys and I will need faith more than ever to raise them right.

Whenever I encounter a difficult time or an unforeseen obstacle, I often pray and ask for guidance. I'm not afraid to ask for help; these are the times when I need it most.

When friends ask me for advice, I almost always point them back inward and ask if they spend any time in prayer. God will give them a much better insight than I can. If they spend time in sincere prayer, I believe that they will receive the guidance they need.

It's exciting to think about what can be accomplished with enough faith. It seems that the opportunities are endless. I pray that you will find the faith you need to accomplish your dreams. Here are a few stories from others who have done just that.

*"Faith can be spiritual.
It can also mean believing
in yourself or the employees
of your company.
Whatever your interpretation,
faith is significant because
it defines both who you are
and the values you hold."*

Clint Arnoldus
President and Chief Executive Officer
CENTRAL PACIFIC BANK

POW - GBA

Captain Jerry Coffee (USN Ret.), Chief Executive Officer, Coffee Enterprises

Part of my 28-year career as a naval officer was spent as a prisoner of war. I was a Navy pilot and was shot down over the country of North Vietnam, captured, and spent the next seven years and nine days there.

I felt that surviving the experience—as most of my friends did—wasn't anything extraordinary. The real mission was not only to live through the experience, but to return with honor. That became our mission, our goal.

Having survived the experience, I came home with a very strong feeling of responsibility to capitalize on the credibility that accrued through the survival experience. I used public speaking as my vehicle to spread the message. Basically, my message was simple. I wanted to plant the seed of belief in people's minds that if it had somehow been them in prison all those years, they too would have survived.

There's nothing extraordinary about me, really. With the same training and orientation going in, others would survive, too. When people believe that to be true—and hopefully I help them to believe a little bit—then it can change their perspective on all challenges in their lives, whether they be personal or professional setbacks, financial difficulties or physical limitations. The feedback that I have received over the years has convinced me that it has been a productive effort, and for me it has been very gratifying.

Honestly, I think that the prisoner of war experience was my greatest challenge. To be able to stay focused for seven years. To keep faith for seven years.

Captain Jerry Coffee is a retired Navy pilot, who was captured during the Vietnam conflict and spent seven years and nine days as a prisoner of war (POW) in North Vietnam, mostly in solitary confinement. He was awarded the Distinguished Flying Cross in 1962 for flying low-level reconnaissance missions over Cuba, taking the photos ultimately used by the United States UN ambassador to prove the existence of Soviet missiles. In a poll of corporate meeting planners, Captain Coffee was selected as one of America's Top 10 speakers as well as one of the Million Dollar Round Table's Top 12 most popular, highest-rated platform speakers for the past 20 years. His numerous civilian awards include the George Washington Honor Medal from the Freedom Foundation at Valley Forge.

To stay close to my greatest source of strength, my God. The first two English words that I saw scratched on the wall of my cell by another American who'd been there before me was a little formula: "God = Strength." For me, that really worked. I was totally alone, and I could always find a little bit more strength when I needed it. That was the primary key to surviving the most challenging experience of my life.

When I was put into prison and the reality began to set in, I thought, "Wait a minute. This is supposed to happen to the other guy, not to me. Why me?"

The real turning point came when my prayers—and there were a lot of them—changed from, "Why me, God?" to "Show me, God."

"Show me what I'm supposed to do with this. What are you preparing me for? What am I supposed to learn from this experience? Help me to use it to go home, whenever that might be, as a better, stronger, smarter person in every possible way. To go home as a better naval officer, to go home as a better Christian, to go home as a better American citizen, to go home as a better husband, father and friend; every possible way help me to use this time productively."

Just knowing that there was a purpose—that there was something to build toward and that every day wasn't just a void or a vacuum in my life—was a major turning point.

One of the things that always inspired me in that prison environment was the way that fellow American prisoners tried to take care of each other. When the man in the cell next to you was down and hurting, or was being punished for four or five weeks with his ankles locked in the ankle stocks at the foot of his concrete slab and his hands manacled behind him, we'd get up to our walls frequently and "tap" GB to him, which means "God bless." He knew that it also meant, "Be tough, babe. Hang in there. I love you, and I'm praying for you." You bet we were.

Then, each night when things would quiet down before we'd go to sleep, we'd tap to the guy in the next cell.

GN … "Good Night."

GB … "God Bless."

GBA … "God bless America."

Every single night; we put that kind of trust, faith and care in one another.

I KNOW THAT ALL THINGS WORK TOGETHER
FOR GOOD TO THOSE WHO LOVE GOD
AND ARE CALLED ACCORDING TO HIS PURPOSE.
(ROMANS 8:28)

"I always lean on this verse
in the Bible because
no matter what, I know God is
working things together for
my good according to
His plan for my life."

Kate Hogle
President
KWME, INC.

Sometimes It's Destiny

June Jones, Football Head Coach, University of Hawai'i

I close my eyes, pray and tell God what I want and what I need. God says in the book of Philippians, "Have no anxiety about anything, but in everything through prayer and supplication let your requests be made known unto God and the peace which surpasses all human understanding will keep your hearts and mind in Christ."

People ask me all the time, "Do you pray to win a game?" I say, "Yeah, I pray to win a game." God doesn't promise me that we'll win the game, but praying takes away my anxiety. I am at peace while I'm at the game. If you're at peace, you really don't care if you win or lose. You prepare yourself and you do your job. Prayer is how I handle pressure. Prayer is how I handle anxiety.

People say all the time, "How do you stay so calm?" I respond, "Prayer." God has already written the newspaper for the next day. God knows what happened yesterday and he knows what's going to happen tomorrow. He already knows the outcome of the game. Hence, I don't worry about it. My job is to be ready to handle the outcome the right way—win or lose.

I pray when I need help with making big decisions, too. I remember struggling with the choice of leaving the head coaching position of the NFL San Diego Chargers to coach the UH Warriors in Hawai'i, which is something I had always dreamed of doing. I felt like I already knew the answer, but I just needed that extra approval from God.

My close friend Steve Barkowski recalled a moment we shared together in 1977. When we were rookies together in Atlanta, he asked me on a NFL film

June Jones is the head coach of the University of Hawai'i's football team. He has won more games than any other coach in the team's history, and has been twice named Western Athletic Conference Coach of the Year. In 1976, he was a Kodak All-American Quarterback for Portland State University. June played for the Atlanta Falcons NFL team where he later became the Head Coach. He turned down the head coaching position for the NFL San Diego Chargers to fulfill a dream of coaching the University of Hawai'i Warriors. June is the founder of the June Jones Foundation, which is dedicated to improving the quality of life for needy families of children with life-threatening illnesses.

show, "What are you going to do after all this?" I said, "I want to be the head coach of the University of Hawai'i one day."

I don't remember that interview, but I do remember that after playing a game in Hawai'i I said that I wanted to come back and live here.

While I was trying to decide whether I should stay in San Diego as the head coach or go to Hawai'i, I prayed over and over for an answer from God. I asked Him to please guide me and show me. Thinking about this gets me a little emotional, but I remember saying a prayer that night.

The San Diego Chargers offered me a three-year contract for millions of dollars to stay as the Chargers' coach. After saying my prayer that night, I remember feeling that I shouldn't stay because the Chargers had drafted a quarterback that I didn't really believe could play.

Still hesitant, I called UH sportscaster Artie Wilson and my agent, Leigh Steinberg.

They suggested, "Well, why don't you ask for a whole bunch of more money and more years?" So, I hung up the phone and thought about it.

I called up the Chargers' general manager, Bobby Beathard, and I said, "Bobby, you know what? I want five years and I need $2 million more." It came to about $7.5 million over a five-year contract.

"I don't know if we can do that," Bobby said, "but I'll get back to you." That was at about 1 a.m., so I hung up the phone and I said a prayer. I figured that their response would be my answer.

Bobby called back in about one hour. He said, "Done."

I figured that was the answer to my prayer, but I still didn't feel good about it.

Hawai'i's Jim Donovan, Hugh Yoshida, Ed Wong and Edison Miyawaki were supposed to meet with me the next morning at 9 a.m. I had gone as far as to write a check to cover all their expenses for coming to California, but now I was going to tell them that I was not going to take the job.

I felt obligated to them, so as a resolution I planned to make a donation to the UH program. As I walked into the meeting, my agent said, "You know, June, I've heard you talk about Hawai'i for 25 years. I think you really need to go through with that interview."

We all sat down and in about five minutes into it, I knew that I was supposed to go with UH. I mean, I knew it instantly.

Edison Miyawaki from Hawai'i expressed several times that he didn't really understand how I could leave all this money in San Diego. After the third time the question was raised, Ed Wong said, "Edison, sometimes it's destiny." That was it. Till this day, I remember when he said that. I knew that was my answer to the prayer.

Regardless of taking a huge pay cut, I was ready because I knew that I wouldn't have been put in this position if God didn't think I could handle it. I believe that God gave me this opportunity and brought me here for a reason. It wasn't just about moving locations or winning games, it was about changing lives of the players, the coaches and the fans. They too, changed who I am, and with God's guidance, it has made me a better person.

*"When our lives focus
merely on the here and now,
we tend to lose sight of
the dreams and capacities
God has placed deep within us.
I want to experience everything
the Creator designed me for
and encourage others
to live out the dreams
God has placed within them."*

William Keliʻi Akina
President and Chief Executive Officer
YOUTH FOR CHRIST HAWAIʻI

Finding God from Within

Don Kim, President, Sony Hawai'i Company

I grew up in Korea during World War II and then the Korean War. It was not really a happy time, but I focused on going to school so that I could learn new things. My family wasn't rich, so I appreciate being raised with a set of values that put importance on the simple things in life. I didn't dream of fancy and materialistic things, but rather solutions for how to make things better. Because of the wars, I felt that there needed to be a change in leadership and politics to improve society. I dreamed of ways that everyone could get along and help each other.

Things have changed since then. Society has become better, as we all reach out globally to help each other's communities. Because of this, I no longer dream of getting into politics or becoming president of the United States of America like I did when I was young.

But in my search for peace and social unanimity, I found God. I have served as a deacon for my church for many years. Having the spirit in me helps me to be a better person. Christianity has guided me through my career path.

Don Kim is the president of Sony Hawai'i Company. With Don at the helm, Sony Hawai'i increased its sales by 16 percent from 2004 to 2005. In 2007, Sony set their sales target to $250 million, thanks to the growing demand on the Mainland and PX military markets. Don began his career with Sony in 1970. He is the president of GCS International - Hawai'i Club, and is on the board of East-West Center Foundation and Hawai'i Baptist Academy. In 1996, he received the Medal of Peony from GCS International and Chairman's Award from Sony Corporation in 1998.

I think that being close to God and being able to listen to Him has taught me to listen to others, including customers. I remind my employees to always listen to our clients so that we can understand what they want from us. By listening we can learn how we can deliver and meet their expectations. I also try to listen to my employees as they share their ideas how to make Sony a better place to work, creating a win-win-win situation for the customer, the employees and the company, so we are all happy.

Since God encourages me to make good choices and to do the best that I can, I encourage my employees to do the same. This has allowed me to lead Sony to a $70 million increase and to make our employees happy.

When I decide to leave Sony, I think I will go to seminary school and become a missionary to do some volunteer work.

That is my goal … to continue listening to God's word and help others to be the best they can be.

*"I think
ultimate fulfillment
results from having
a balanced life
with your spouse ...
it is that very worship of God
that helps me love her more."*

Jimmy Yamada, Jr.
Chief Executive Officer
A-1 A-LECTRICIAN

A Greater Purpose

Clint Arnoldus, President and Chief Executive Officer, Central Pacific Bank

Faith and family. These are, and always will be, the cornerstones of my life.

I've been blessed to have spent over 30 years in banking. It's been an exciting, challenging career.

Still, when I come home from work at the end of the day, I enjoy nothing more than spending time with my wife, Lesley, my six children and my twelve grandchildren. They are my foundation. They energize me, sustain me, and rejuvenate me.

Just like my faith does.

Faith and family remind me constantly that there is a greater purpose to life. Material success can and will only take you so far. You can have the biggest houses, the finest cars, the largest paychecks, and still feel pretty empty. Faith and my family remind me about this important precept every single day of my life.

I think this viewpoint helps me get over the bumps in life. It allows me to have a long-term perspective on challenges that may otherwise seem insurmountable.

For example, faith and family played a huge part in my journey towards becoming a CEO. I was an executive vice president for First Interstate Bank of Nevada. Above me were two bank presidents—one ran northern Nevada and the other one managed southern Nevada. It was a given that one of the presidents would eventually get the CEO job, so I never thought that I would get my shot.

But one day, an unexpected opportunity came up.

The CEO was scheduled to speak at an annual Las Vegas event, where business leaders from the community talk to large convention groups. About 4,000

Clint Arnoldus is the president and CEO of Central Pacific Financial Corp., which is the fourth-largest financial institution in Hawai'i, with $5.5 billion in assets. In the past, Clint served as chairman and CEO of First Interstate Bank of Nevada and Community Bank in Pasadena, California. Clint serves on the Board of the Chamber of Commerce of Hawai'i, Hawai'i Business Roundtable and the University of Hawai'i Foundation. He donates his time to serve the YWCA, March of Dimes and the Shriners Hospital for Children.

people attended the event annually and the CEO of First Interstate Bank of Nevada, which was the biggest bank in Nevada, presented the financial portion of the event.

The morning of the event, the CEO called in sick! He was so sick that he couldn't even get out of bed. He called in at 8 a.m. and his presentation was to start at 10 a.m. The bank approached the two presidents above me but both declined requests to take the president's place. So, they came to me and asked me if I would do it.

By 9 a.m. I agreed I would.

A half hour before the presentation, I looked over the CEO's presentation and decided I had to start from scratch. I only had about 20 minutes to pull something together. I was extremely nervous, but I focused on the task at hand. Fortunately, everything just clicked and the presentation was well received. It was a blessing that the bank's board of directors were in the audience, because when the CEO position opened up 60 days later, they unexpectedly offered me the position.

This was a once-in-a-lifetime opportunity. Both my faith and my family—who believed in me from day one—helped pull me through that day.

Another example of faith and family seeing me through tough times was during the merger between Central Pacific Bank and City Bank. When I first got recruited to be the CEO of Central Pacific Bank, it was obvious to me that the bank needed to merge with another small bank to be more effective in Hawai'i's competitive banking environment. Of course, this would mean change, and many people don't like change. However, I believe change comes bearing gifts.

The merger was a challenge for me, both personally and professionally, but I tried to stay focused on the greater good.

One day, after a difficult day at work during the merger, my son Brad, who was a junior in high school, came up to me when I walked in the door and gave me a big hug and said, "Dude, are you OK?"

It was very heartwarming. While going through tough times as a professional, it really strengthened me knowing that faith and family were beside me, ready to hold me up and support me.

When Brad hugged me that day, I knew that everything would be OK.

And it was.

"So much of life is about faith;
faith in others, faith in one's self,
faith in justice and faith in God.
Without faith
one would be paralyzed
by indecision and lack of hope."

T. Michael May
President & Chief Executive Officer
HAWAIIAN ELECTRIC COMPANY, INC.

Desert Storm

Admiral R.J. "Zap" Zlatoper (USN Ret.), Trustee, The Estate of James Campbell

Some people say, "I'm a spiritual person, but I don't really have a particular faith."

That doesn't compute. Religion and faith are items you have to work at. If you want to have a physically fit body, you eat right and exercise regularly. If you want to be mentally strong, you study and educate yourself. If you want to be spiritually grounded, you have to embrace a faith and spend time developing your spirituality. I don't think you can be a successful businessperson in the long run if you're not well rounded physically, mentally and spiritually.

After successful careers in the high-tech industry and in the U.S. Navy, Admiral R.J. "Zap" Zlatoper assumed his position as the 24th trustee of the Estate of James Campbell in 2000. In the private and public sectors, Zlatoper has served for more than 10 years as the chief executive of large organizations. He served as co-chairman of the board and CEO of Sanchez Computer Associates, Inc., a banking software company rated 45th in *Forbes* magazine list of the 200 best small companies in the United States. Before joining Sanchez, he completed a distinguished naval career. His final assignment was Commander in Chief of the U.S. Pacific Fleet, the world's largest naval command, which encompasses half the Earth's surface and includes more than 190 ships, 1,600 aircraft and 200,000 personnel, with an operating budget of $5 billion per year.

One of my most memorable military stories about spirituality occurred at the beginning of Desert Storm. As Rear Admiral, I was the Commander of the Ranger Battle Group and the Surface Warfare Commander in the Persian Gulf. In the Battle Group were eight ships, including an aircraft carrier, 75 aircraft, two cruisers, three destroyers, a submarine and a supply/ammunition ship with 8,000 men and women on board. I was charged with the responsibility of eliminating the Iraqi Navy (yes, they had one).

Although I had served in the Vietnam War, I had never before been present at the start of combat. The night before hostilities, everyone wanted to talk to the chaplain. It was a dramatic change from one week earlier when some sailors and Marines were saying, "I don't need to commit to anything having to do with religion. I'm not into that kind of thing."

Suddenly they realized they were about to face the beginning of a war and they were confronted with a dangerous unknown. It was life threatening to everyone. It reminded me of that World War II adage that "there are no atheists in foxholes."

I remember the chaplain that first night at a church service explaining that sometimes there are things in your life that are beyond your control, times when one must say, "I have to turn to a higher force for support."

One of the most concerned individuals that evening was the commanding officer of one of our aviation squadrons. He came up to me as he was about to fly his first combat mission and said, "Admiral, I'm very worried and frightened here. I'm the commanding officer and I don't know that I have the courage or commitment to go and do this."

I told him, "You and I have known each other for a long time and you have a couple of hundred people relying on you, looking for your leadership. The best advice I can offer you is to go back and pray for strength and courage. If you can't execute your task after that, come back and talk to me because if you're not going to do your part in this war, we're going to handle it someway differently."

The commander left and later that night went out and flew his mission, leading a flight of four aircraft. I didn't hear anything further from him until after he returned from his second mission. He came back to me and said, "God made all the difference."

He turned to God and faith to acknowledge that there are some things you can't control. And I think we all have moments in our lives where we say, "This problem is more than I can personally handle alone."

In a related way, faith had helped me throughout my operational life in the Navy. I commanded one aviation squadron for two years, two carrier air wings for three years, and one carrier battle group for almost two years. During that period, we had no operational aircraft losses (no aircraft lost due to crashes or accidents), which is highly unusual, if not unprecedented. The absence of operational losses during years of intense flying operations at sea was testimony to the strong commitment of the men and women who worked with me to doing things correctly and precisely while still operating near the limits of their abilities. Along with thorough training, I believe the knowledge they were serving the American people and being true to their faith were key factors to our success.

It may be subjective, but in my experience the people who get through such experiences most gracefully are those who pray or have faith. Along those lines, I have this strong belief that you ought not pray for "things," such as a military victory or success in business. The sale that kick-started our high-tech software business, Sanchez Computer Associates, was a contract with a global financial institution to buy and use our software. That put us on the map. While we were courting them and making presentations, our people came up to me and said, "We've done everything we can, we don't know what else we can do."

Somebody replied, "Well, I guess all we can do now is pray."

Then I said, "Yes, we can pray, but we're not going to pray that we get the contract. We're going to pray to do our absolute best in this undertaking."

I think that's where faith comes into play. You don't ask for something physical from your Lord, your God, or whoever your Divine Power is. You ask Him to give you the strength and wisdom to do the right thing, and then have faith that He will handle things that are beyond your control in a way that you may not always understand. When we leave it up to God, it is always taken care of.

*"God won't give you
more than you can handle.
He may close a door,
but he's going to
open a window."*

Rebecca Parker
President
M. DYER & SONS

Ask Him

William Keli'i Akina, President and Chief Executive Officer, Youth for Christ

There are lots of occasions when I've banded together with other people to do good for the community, but I am convinced prayer and faith are what have really made all the difference. Perhaps the most memorable time was an ambitious project designed to bless more than 400,000 families. I don't need to go into details, but this was in response to the tragic events of September 11, 2001.

We were down to the wire on the project I had been asked to chair, and the make-or-break issue was a sizeable financial gap. Large sums of money from generous individuals had poured in, but we still needed exactly $103,000 more. Without that amount, the project would have to be scaled back, and many local communities would be left out.

William Keli'i Akina is president and CEO of Youth for Christ Hawai'i, the largest interdenominational youth ministry in Hawai'i. He oversees the work of Campus Life, Fellowship of Christian Athletes, YFC for Parents, and the Center for Tomorrow's Leaders, which inspires exceptional youth to pursue careers of public service. Keli'i was chairman and CEO of an historic interdenominational coalition of 191 churches, for which he led a successful $1.7 million fundraising effort following September 11, 2001. In 2002, Keli'i was appointed a Pacific Century Fellow. Keli'i is also an Adjunct Professor of humanities and philosophy at Hawai'i Pacific University and holds degrees from the University of Hawai'i and Northwestern University.

Danny Casey, one of my close associates, and I were the last ones in my office making phone calls. We called everyone we knew whom we thought could help out. The deadline to confirm or cancel the project with our Mainland partners was looming. We were so close to the amount needed, but we just couldn't pull it off. Sadly, although we had been praying, asking God to open the doors, we now had to make a dreaded call to cancel portions of the project. With that in mind, I decided to try one last person.

The man I planned to call was someone whom I had recently said "no" to, so it wasn't going to be an easy call for me. Yet I knew he had resources. He had asked a favor and offered to pay for all the production and distribution costs of a CD-album my organization wanted to distribute in Hawai'i's schools if we would feature his son and his son's band on the album. Unfortunately, our staff and a focus group of teenagers decided against featuring his son's music, so I apologetically turned down his request and his money. Now I was going to call the same man at the eleventh hour to ask him to make a contribution!

Danny and I stopped and prayed: "Dear Lord, please provide … for your glory!"

Then I dialed.

The man answered the phone and, before I could even start to explain why I called, he said he needed to tell me something. So I let him go first.

He said God had "told" him to give us the amount of money he would have spent on the album we refused to put his son on.

That amount was $100,000.

We were floored.

It was just minutes from the deadline and we were virtually at the amount needed. Yet, I was still torn inside. Should I go with the amount raised so far or keep trying to raise the remaining $3,000? After all, God had provided the big amount. Was it worth asking someone for the small amount too?

OK, so we thought of one more person, and I called half-heartedly.

This time when the other party said, "I already gave what I could," I prepared myself to hear, "I'm sorry."

Instead, the gentleman continued, "But now I can give $3,000. Can you use it?"

Without having hinted a word to this man as to what had happened in the prior call, we were offered the exact dollar amount that we needed. Danny and I found ourselves on our knees, with tears streaming down our faces. I really don't know what impacted me more, the $100,000 or the final $3,000. In retrospect, I think it was the smaller amount because that showed me, in precise detail, that this was no mere coincidence. God was in control all along. And I learned a powerful lesson.

No amount is too big and no amount is too small for God.

My job is just to have faith and ask Him.

*"The last three years
have really strengthened
my personal relationship
with God. When I came
into office, I saw first-hand
how divisive and intolerant
politics could be, and my faith
gave me the strength to
forgive and reach out
across the political divide
to better serve all the people
of this state."*

James R. "Duke" Aiona, Jr.
Lieutenant Governor
STATE OF HAWAI'I

Paradoxical Commandments

Dr. Kent M. Keith, Chief Executive Officer, Greenleaf Center for Servant-Leadership

I think faith is really relevant to how we should behave, how we should live our lives, understanding what's worth doing and why we should do it. For me, I believe we should be in the world, but not of the world. By that I mean we need to be fully engaged, we need to be active, we need to use the talents and gifts we are given, we need to do the best we can do, we need to be as successful as we can be—but we don't have to buy into all the secular commercial values that are around us. We don't have to seek power, wealth and fame as though they are the answer.

From the perspective of being *in* the world but not *of* the world—power, wealth, and fame are tools. They are tools to be used in loving and helping others. So when you have access to resources, you should use them to serve God and live your faith in an appropriate way. It's not about self-denial or self-sacrifice, it's about self-fulfillment. Everything we know about power, wealth and fame tells us that in themselves, they don't really satisfy us. They aren't fulfilling, they aren't really that meaningful. The meaning comes from using them to love and help others.

I was just very fortunate to grow up with people who understood this. And it connected with what I was learning at church. I remember the struggle I had in high school Sunday School with what happened to Jesus on Good Friday. To me, Good Friday just seemed ugly and awful. On that day the world did all the

Dr. Kent M. Keith is the author of the best selling *Anyway: The Paradoxical Commandments*, which has received worldwide recognition. He has practiced law, served as a cabinet member for the state of Hawai'i, developed a high-tech park, held a six-year term as president at Chaminade University, served as a senior vice president for the YMCA of Honolulu, and is now the CEO of the Greenleaf Center for Servant-Leadership in Indiana. Dr. Keith has an eclectic educational background—after graduating from Roosevelt High School in Honolulu, he studied at Harvard, where he received a Bachelor of Arts in Government; then he went to Oxford as a Rhodes Scholar and earned a bachelor's and master's in philosophy and politics; then he traveled to Japan to study Japanese at Waseda University in Tokyo. He returned to Hawai'i to earn his J.D. from the University of Hawai'i; and years later, a stint at the University of Southern California earned him his Ed.D.

terrible things it could do to Jesus. I just didn't want to think about it, it was just too painful.

It took me a long time to realize, as millions of people have realized, that what the world did to Jesus on that day was only half the story. The other half of the story is how Jesus responded to what the world did to him. His response was really astonishing. It was really breathtaking, because his response was to love people anyway, to forgive people anyway, to save people anyway. That idea of doing the right thing anyway, being who you are supposed to be, and living the way you are supposed to live anyway—that was a huge breakthrough for me. It was an idea that really influenced my life. And it changed my view of Good Friday from an awful day of defeat to a day of triumph. Good Friday was a triumph over life, and then Easter Sunday was a triumph over death.

The Paradoxical Commandments
By Dr. Kent M. Keith

People are illogical, unreasonable and self-centered.
Love them anyway.
If you do good, people will accuse you of selfish ulterior motives.
Do good anyway.
And if you are successful, you will win false friends and true enemies.
Succeed anyway.
The good you do today will be forgotten tomorrow.
Do good anyway.
Honesty and frankness make you vulnerable.
Be honest and frank anyway.
The biggest men and women with the biggest ideas can be shot down
     by the smallest men and women with the smallest minds.
Think big anyway.
People favor underdogs but follow only top dogs.
Fight for a few underdogs anyway.
What you spend years building may be destroyed overnight.
Build anyway.
People really need help but may attack you if you do help them.
Help people anyway.
Give the world the best you have and you'll get kicked in the teeth.
Give the world the best you have anyway.

*"Enjoy life.
Life is beautiful
and the more experiences
that you have,
the richer life becomes."*

Constance H. Lau
President and Chief Executive Officer
HAWAIIAN ELECTRIC INDUSTRIES, INC.
Chairman, President and Chief Executive Officer
AMERICAN SAVINGS BANK

EPILOGUE

Evan Leong, Chief Executive Officer, Greater Good Inc.

Steve Jobs, co-founder of Apple and former CEO of Pixar, compares our experiences in life with connecting dots. Here's how he put it in a commencement speech at Stanford University in 2005: *"You can't connect the dots looking forward; you can only connect them looking backwards. So you have to trust that the dots will somehow connect in your future. You have to trust in something—your gut, destiny, life, karma, whatever. This approach has never let me down, and it has made all the difference in my life ... Sometimes life hits you in the head with a brick. Don't lose faith. I'm convinced that the only thing that kept me going was that I loved what I did. You've got to find what you love. And that is as true for your work as it is for your lovers. Your work is going to fill a large part of your life, and the only way to be truly satisfied is to do what you believe is great work. And the only way to do great work is to love what you do. If you haven't found it yet, keep looking. Don't settle. As with all matters of the heart, you'll know when you find it. And, like any great relationship, it just gets better and better as the years roll on. So keep looking until you find it. Don't settle."*

I attended Punahou School, one of the most prestigious academic institutions in Hawai'i. My parents worked really hard to get me in and keep me in. I was hyperactive and had a hard time fitting in with all the smart kids. I couldn't stay as still as they could and early on was diagnosed with Attention Deficit Hyperactivity Disorder.

In high school I felt absolutely overwhelmed. Paying attention in class had always been hard for me, which meant that I had to work harder at exam time to catch up. On top of that I got really sick, which took me out of school for months. At the end of my sophomore year exams I was exhausted. I wanted to move out of Punahou and go to a public school where the workload would be less demanding. I felt that I was a waste of money and didn't belong. But I knew that my parents would kick me out of the house if I did, so transferring was out of the question.

After exams, I met up with my close friend, Kekoa, to begin our summer break. When I asked how his exams had gone, he smiled and told me they were easy. When I prodded him further, I found out that exams had been easy for Kekoa because he didn't have many. He was taking several art classes and just the bare requirements for academic courses.

I immediately adopted his model and registered for just about every art class I could find. This included the likes of Visual Composition I/II, Drawing I/II, Clay Handbuilding I, Glass Blowing I/II and Jewelry I/II. My mom thought I was going nowhere with this and only tolerated it because she wanted me to graduate. My art classes were the only classes keeping my GPA up.

What started as a way to get out of academic courses soon became something I really got into. Art allowed me to create. It was no longer about memorization. It was about imagination and execution. Could I come up with something in my mind and use raw materials to bring it to life? Building something special out of the ordinary fascinated me. I didn't realize at the time just how deep an impact these courses would have on my future.

As an entrepreneur, I get satisfaction and compensation from what I create, not what I can memorize and regurgitate. The process of starting a company is much the same as taking bits of metal, solder and stones to create a beautiful piece of jewelry. It's really no different from taking a lump of clay and some paint and fashioning a beautiful vase or sculpture, or taking broken glass and heating it, blowing air into it and making a set of drinking glasses. In art, we take nothing and make it into something. Isn't that what we're trying to do with our lives?

Says University of Hawai'i president David McClain: "What I was really struck by about the arts is how much the education in the arts helps in the creative impulse when it comes to starting a business. If you think of an artist facing a blank canvas, or a dancer facing an empty stage, that emptiness represents lots of risks. As you put yourself out there, drawing something on a canvas or dancing on an empty stage, that risk-taking mindset is the core of expressing yourself if you're in the arts … it was completely aligned with my interest in entrepreneurship because the risk-taking behavior is what you want to encourage."

I honestly believe that the foundation of my tolerance to risk and the ability to create were developed in those art classes at Punahou. Conventional wisdom might say that they were a waste of time and money but, being unconventional, I don't feel they were a waste of either my time or my parents' hard-earned money.

In 2000, Kari and I decided to move back to Hawai'i from California where we were working at the time. Due to unforseen circumstances, we returned home with broken spirits, small bank accounts and low confidence.

At the same time a good friend of mine was earning a great six-figure income as a software programmer. His business as a contractor was booming, and he could work from home and spend time with his family. I realized then that I didn't have deep expertise in anything. I had quit college after my second year. I had worked in sales and marketing for eight years but really had nothing to show for it. A lot of my friends were graduating from law and medical school and ready to start "real" careers. I was pretty depressed. I felt like a loser. The only thing I could think of was to go back and finish college, which I did.

A funny thing happened in the process. Kari and I decided to start our own company, Bubble Tea Supply, which ultimately became a major success. During that time I realized something. As an entrepreneur, my jack-of-all-trades-master-of-none background became a great strength. When I tied that together with creativity and risk-taking, our business took off. I may not have been an expert in all the requisite areas, but I understood a lot of things and hired people who could do those jobs much better than I could. My sales background allowed me to negotiate win-win deals that are still in place today and to increase our sales revenues. My perceived weaknesses were really strengths. The determining factor was time. It just took a while for the dots to connect.

I didn't realize it back then, but the dots had always been connecting. I was always on the path. I just didn't know it. Chances are that you are already on your path, too. Your dots are connecting, whether you realize it or not. Keep following your purpose and passion. Give back, overcome adversity and build your relationships, your family and your faith, and the connections will show themselves in due time.

You have the ability to create a better life. Make your life a work of art. Create your life to make a difference.

ABOUT THE AUTHORS

Evan Leong attended Punahou School and graduated cum laude from Hawai'i Pacific University, where he was the first recipient of the Distinguished Certificate of Business Excellence. Evan is also a member of the Delta Mu Delta Honor Society and was the 2007 recipient of the Paul C.T. Loo Young Alumni Award from Hawai'i Pacific University. He obtained his Executive Masters of Business Administration from the University of Hawai'i at Mānoa in 2005.

In 2006, Evan was recognized by *Pacific Business News* in its "Forty under 40" business award, and selected as one of Hawai'i's 2006 Top High Tech Leaders on behalf of the Pacific Technology Foundation and the Technology News Network. In 2007, he and his wife, Kari, won the state and regional Small Business Administration (SBA) Small Business Journalist of the Year Award.

Evan coaches for the University of Hawai'i Pacific Asian Center for Entrepreneurship Business Plan Competition to develop future entrepreneurs. He is on the board of directors for the University of Hawai'i Alumni Association and University Community Partnership. Evan is the chairman of the City and County of Honolulu's Month in Chinatown Celebration. He also serves on the Boy Scouts of America committee of the Aloha Council's Learning for Life Program, which teaches character building to Hawai'i's youth. Evan was chosen in 2005 to participate in Mayor Mufi Hannemann's Pacific Century Fellows (PCF). PCF is a year-long leadership development program modeled after the White House Fellows.

Evan also co-founded Bubble Tea Supply in 2001 with Kari. He is married with two boys and enjoys stand-up paddle surfing and kite surfing.

Kari Leong holds a bachelor's degree in Journalism and Elementary School Educaton, plus a master's degree in Administration, Curriculum and Instruction, both from Gonzaga University in Spokane, Washington. Graduating cum laude for her degrees, she is also a certified elementary teacher and a member of the Educator's Honor Society, Kappa Delta Pi.

In 2006, Kari was recognized by *Pacific Business News* in its "Forty under 40" business award. She was the female winner in the 2007 *Hawaii Business* magazine "Fittest CEO" Contest. Also in 2007, Kari and Evan won the state and regional Small Business Administration (SBA) Small Business Journalist of the Year Award.

Kari was a semifinalist judge for the University of Hawai'i Pacific Asian Center for Entrepreneurship Business Plan Competition designed to develop new entrepreneurs and small businesses. She is an active participant with Mid-Pacific Institute's Alumni Association, serving as a class representative and chaperone for Project Graduations. Kari is a member of the Boy Scouts of America Committee of the Aloha Council's Learning for Life Program, which teaches character building to Hawai'i's youth. She serves on the board of directors for the Women's Fund of Hawai'i and is the In-Service Coordinator for Honolulu's Meals on Wheels program to provide training for the site's volunteers.

Kari was chosen in 2006 to participate in Mayor Mufi Hannemann's Pacific Century Fellows (PCF). PCF is a year-long leadership development program modeled after the White House Fellows.

Kari also co-founded Bubble Tea Supply in 2001 with Evan. She is married with two boys and enjoys shopping and exercise.

INDEX BY NAME

INDEX BY COMPANY

To order and
for more information please visit:
www.GreaterGoodBooks.com

Or call
808-945-1111

*Corporate, bulk, church and fund-raising
discounts available.*